Project Mushroom

Project Mushroom

A Modern Guide to Growing Fungi

By

Caley Bros.

F FRANCES
LINCOLN

Contents

Introduction

Our mushroom-growing journey began back in 2018, when we both decided to move towards more plant-based diets. Our father had sadly passed away from cancer that year, and it was this devastating diagnosis that made us reevaluate our relationship with food.

As we think many of us do, we started by simply substituting meat for more vegetables – but there was something missing, and we were often left unsatisfied. When growing up, our family meals had been rich, hearty and bursting with flavour; we now wanted to rediscover some of that magic. Not being the types to give up easily, we started researching and found some interesting cookbooks that introduced us to the power of the edible mushroom. Of course, we knew about the button mushrooms that we had cooked with multiple times before, but now we were discovering varieties that we'd never even heard of. They promised new and exciting flavours and dense meaty textures, and were packed full of protein, fibre, B vitamins and minerals. The magic we were looking for.

Eagerly perusing pages, we soon learnt that mushrooms could be marinated, sliced, pickled, barbecued and dried. They could become stocks and sauce thickeners, seasonings for both sweet or savoury baking, and so much more. Unfortunately, back in 2018, for us anything beyond the chestnut, button or portobello mushroom was difficult to find, especially fresh. What were deemed as 'gourmet mushrooms' were mostly being shipped around the world, often sealed in plastic packaging. So huge carbon footprint notwithstanding, the mushroom themselves were often underwhelming and nowhere near as substantial as the ones we'd seen pictured in our cookbooks.

When growing up, we had witnessed first-hand the wonders of home-grown mushrooms. Our parents kept a kit under the kitchen sink, and every few days there would be another handful of button mushrooms ready to harvest. Fast forward thirty years and online learning gave us access to a whole new world of information. We discovered that gourmet mushrooms, such as oyster mushrooms, are easy to grow yourself. We bought our first bag of spawn and started growing for ourselves, harvesting our first oyster mushrooms just eight weeks later.

In 2019, we took our fascination with mushrooms to the next level. A continuing curiosity and constant requests from friends, family and

colleagues for a taste of our delicious produce showed us there was a huge appetite for locally sourced and home-grown mushrooms. Having taken a break from our careers to raise families and care for our dad, the transition from growing mushrooms for ourselves to working together and making Caley Brothers our own business felt completely natural – but also remarkable, given we didn't get on too well as kids!

We've since had the privilege of working with Kew Gardens, where we installed a stunning mushroom bed under a magnificent magnolia tree within their newly refurbished Kitchen Garden. Within the bed we wanted to demonstrate a variety of growing techniques that would produce an array of different and delicious mushrooms. All of the projects that we installed, you can find within the pages of this book.

But why 'Caley Brothers' and not sisters?! The Caley Brothers' brand was first established well before we (and even our parents) were born. Back in the 1950s, our grandad and his brother started a grocery delivery service. They bought a huge white truck and decked the inside out with shelving and a set of steps. Every morning, they would drive to London and load up with fresh fruit and vegetables from Borough and Brentford markets. They'd then tour the new housing estates of Molesey in Surrey, delivering fresh produce direct to people's doors. Before long, they were able to open permanent shop premises on Molesey High Street. For many years, their successful family business continued until the shop they leased was sold, and they decided to pursue a new venture.

In 2000, while passing the old shop premises, our grandparents stopped to watch as an old shopfront was pulled down from what had been their beloved greengrocer. To their amazement, it exposed the original hand-painted Caley Brothers sign hidden beneath; that's how we got to see the original Caley Brothers branding for the first time. With their blessing, we re-established the family name and now use the original brand for our own business. The name also honours our father; his loss left a massive void in our lives. Growing mushrooms has brought us back together, and it's what keeps us united in his absence.

We have since outgrown the garage in our father's garden, where we first took the plunge into mushroom farming. As interest and demand has grown, we've expanded – introducing more varieties, all on locally sourced substrates and often using by-products of local industries. The quick and simple growing process of edible mushrooms has never failed to bring us joy, and it's the knowledge that so many of us can do this ourselves that drives us to share what we've discovered so far. Mushroom growing is still a mystery to so many, but we've learnt that, if you understand the basics, there are many fun and curious ways you can grow mushrooms at home.

At Caley Brothers, we're passionate about all aspects of growing good-quality, sustainable and delicious mushrooms. We want to get as many of you out there growing mushrooms too! This is why we've written this book.

In the following pages we provide you with the tools and advice to get started without any of the jargon or complex equipment, and whatever your available space and ability. We hope we can inspire you to give it a go, and then to keep on growing.

Lorraine and Jodie Caley

Part 1

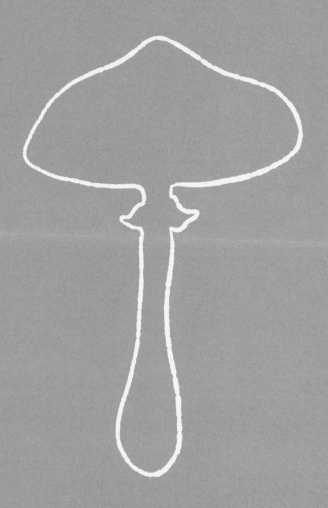

Introducing
Mushrooms

Why Grow Mushrooms?

Many of us will remember the simple growing projects of our school days; watching broad beans grow in jars and cress seeds sprout on beds of cottonwool stuffed into eggshells. For some of us this progressed to propagating geranium stems and planting our first bulbs. And in adulthood we find our desire to nurture extends to an indulgence in houseplants and the planning of ideal flowerbeds and vegetable patches. Yet very few of us have ever been shown how to grow mushrooms! Despite it being incredibly simple – whether using a ready to grow kit or simply mixing a handful of spawn into used coffee grounds, you can be harvesting your first crop of mushrooms in a matter of weeks. But why grow mushrooms in the first place?

They can be grown all year round, and almost anywhere

It might be surprising to hear, but mushrooms are perfect for indoor growing. They make great house plants and there are a great many varieties of edible mushrooms that can be grown at home throughout the year. Once you've finished harvesting your summer veg, you can grow mushrooms on your vegetable beds for the perfect winter harvest. You can even grow mushrooms on logs, leaving them on your balcony or in your front garden to fruit. Please do bear in mind that fungi produce spores that may cause allergies. If you live with someone with a serious illness or who is immunocompromized, we advise finding an alternative location to try the projects.

They grow incredibly quickly

Once incubated and ready to go, some mushrooms double in size every 12–24 hours and can be ready to harvest in just a week. If you're growing outdoors, be quick to harvest or you may find your garden minibeasts get to them first.

They're super low-maintenance

After a little upfront effort, mushrooms pretty much take care of themselves. In most outdoor mushroom-growing projects, all you have to do is make sure that the substrate is well-shaded and doesn't dry out. While some outdoor projects may take a few months to inoculate, long-term fruiting is more than enough reward. Once you've finished growing your mushrooms and their fruiting life is over, you can compost every element and reap the nutritional benefits in your next gardening project.

They're delicious!

All home-grown produce tastes better, and mushrooms are no exception – the flavour, texture and aroma of your freshly harvested mushrooms will blow you away, and inspire you to go on and grow more.

The Future of Growing Mushrooms

Mushrooms have been gathered, foraged and consumed since at least the Stone Age. Evidence includes mushroom spores found in the teeth of The Red Lady of El Mirón, whose remains were unearthed by a team on archaeologists in Spain in 2010 – she is believed to be around 19,000 years old.

Mushroom cultivation is likely to have been undertaken for centuries, if not more. However, the first recorded mushroom cultivation was in Western cultures c.1650. It involved a strain of *Agaricus bisporus*; the classic mushroom that we see today in most supermarkets. Although originally grown in fields, it was soon discovered that they could also be grown in the dark. After that, the farming of these common mushrooms moved into caves and underground tunnels – the cool, damp conditions were perfect growing conditions, and allowed for production to be easily managed year-round. Pioneered by the French, this indoor technique was quickly adopted by other countries and to this day remains the most popular method for cultivating supermarket staples including cremini, button and portobello. Fun fact for you – all of these mushrooms, in fact, derive from that same mushroom species, *Agaricus bisporus*. They are simply harvested at different stages of their development.

Nowadays, low-tech and modern cultivation processes mean we are seeing an increase in smaller urban farms growing a larger variety of stunning and delicious mushrooms, including pink and yellow oyster mushrooms, lion's mane and nameko. All of these mushrooms thrive on agricultural by-products such as sawdust, soyhulls and used coffee grounds. By embracing the circular economy, small producers are reducing a substantial amount of waste from going to landfill, advocating a green and sustainable approach to farming, and all the while supplying their local area with fresh, good-quality produce.

It is well known that some types of mushrooms have been consumed not just for their flavour and nutritional benefits, but for their mind-altering properties. The 'magic mushroom' is a common name bestowed on a family of mushrooms (of nearly 200 species!) that contain the psychoactive chemicals psilocybin and psilocin. Magic mushrooms have been used in religious and spiritual ceremonies for thousands of years – we know this because they're depicted in many forms of ancient sculpture and spiritual artworks around the world. They can alter a person's state of consciousness when consumed, and heighten emotions and senses, allowing people to experience a sense of mental and emotional clarity.

Unregulated recreational use of magic mushrooms led, in the 1970s, to a worldwide ban on the sale, production and consumption of all psilocybin mushrooms. This thwarted any research into the medicinal benefits of mushrooms over the following decades. Today, research levels are on the rise again, with interesting new studies looking into the benefits of using certain mushrooms in tandem with specialized counselling as a method of treating mental health disorders, such as clinical depressions and post-traumatic stress disorder (PTSD). However, the recreational use of magical mushrooms is still illegal.

The power of the mushroom is also now making itself known in fashion, retail and building industries. Pioneering production techniques are harnessing the benefits of the mycelium network. Mycelium is the root network of the mushroom; it is incredibly fast-growing and quickly binds together any loose materials in its vicinity, crisscrossing its network of hyphae to create a firm and stable structure with a finish that is soft to the touch as well as water-resistant.

Product developers – from packaging engineers and fashion designers seeking new materials, to builders wanting insulation materials – are looking into ways to harness this incredible natural technology. By creating a mould of the desired form or structure, it is then filled with a mix of loose materials from common agricultural waste including hemp and sawdust and mixed with a specific mushroom spawn. As the spawn grows, it bonds the loose substrate, turning the whole thing white with mycelium in just a matter of days. Once colonized, the substrate is then dried to preserve its shape and to prevent the fruiting of mushrooms. So in the case of packaging, the final product is as versatile and durable as polystyrene, but if added to your compost or buried in the garden will decompose with a matter of weeks. Mycelium products could be the much-needed solution to the problem of many single-use plastic items, and the future of not only food but also fashion and architecture! Watch this space.

Demystifying Mushrooms

At Caley Brothers, we're keen to demystify mushrooms and bring them further into the light; for their stunning forms, easy growth, environmental benefits and culinary rewards. We're pleased to see an exciting increase in the fascination for mushrooms and other types of fungi. There are huge benefits to getting outdoors and taking a closer look at the natural beauty around us, and mushroom spotting is a brilliant way to do so. There are countless apps now, too, that can help us identify finds without the pressure of picking. You'll start to see that some mushrooms grow in the same spots each year, while others keep us guessing, sporadically popping up overnight, throughout the year.

Friend or foe?

An aversion to mushrooms growing in the wild has been building through generations, caused in part by the rapid expansion of towns and cities and the increase in supermarket shopping. Such stores tend to stock a very basic supply of recognizable and regimented produce year-round. This convenience has led to our detachment from the woods and grasslands that used to supply a bounty of fresh and seasonal edibles. Over time, the unique cultural and culinary knowledge that would have otherwise been passed down through generations has been largely lost, leaving mushrooms in the dark hidden spaces that they grow, and shrouded in mystery and folklore.

Our first encounters with wild mushrooms and other fungi often come in the form of storybooks, many of which depict the colourful but poisonous fly agaric toadstool. Its distinctive, red with white spots stand out against dark undergrowth – it's a powerful first impression of a fruiting fungi. But, of course, such toadstools come with a warning, and we learn to stay well clear. As we get older, stories of toxic fungi linger in our subconscious – how similar they can be to their edible counterparts, and how detrimental they can be to our digestive systems, vital organs or even life itself. Terry Pratchett once said, 'All fungi are edible, some fungi are only edible once.'

Poisonous or not, the appearance of mushrooms can be taken as good signs: of biodiverse conditions and good soil health. They are nature's decomposers – without them, vegetation and detritus would build

up and our soils would become stagnant and depleted. So if you've mushrooms popping up in your potted plants, raised beds or freshly mown law, don't worry – it's no bad thing. It means the mycelium network below ground is thriving, transporting nutrients throughout the soil and helping all your other plants to grow strong and healthy.

Common misconceptions

One of the biggest beliefs surrounding mushrooms is that they grow only in the dark – a hang-up from 'modern day' mushroom cultivation. It's true that your classic cremini, button and portobello varieties will grow in the dark. Large-scale mushroom farms grow them on dense racks of sterilized manure, stacking them high in order to keep production costs down.

But for most mushrooms, light actually helps to initiate fruiting, promotes healthy growth and gives some varieties of mushrooms their depth of colour. An absence of light can sometimes inhibit a mushroom's true form, colour and growth. In fact, cultivated mushrooms are sometimes deliberately exposed to ultraviolet light before being packaged. Such light allows these dark-dwelling mushrooms to become supercharged with vitamin D – a difficult-to-source but vital vitamin. All mushrooms have the potential to produce vitamin D if exposed to direct sunlight. To supercharge your shop-bought mushrooms yourself, simply leave them in the sun for an hour (see page 136).

When Carl Linnaeus invented his binary nomenclature categorization of plants and animals in the eighteenth century, mushrooms were labelled as plants. Only in 1969 were fungi finally given their very own kingdom. It was during this long period of mis-categorization that most of the common terminology around mushrooms was established, and is why we still describe many aspects of fungi in plant terms. In all ways, they're much closer to animals.

A few things set fungi apart from plants: mushrooms don't make their own food as plants do. Instead, they produce enzymes similar to animals, digesting their food before absorbing the nutrients. In animals this process takes place internally, whereas in fungi the enzymes are excreted from their hyphae and their food is broken down externally before being ingested. Mushrooms lack chlorophyll, the natural chemical compound found in plants that is essential for photosynthesis. This is the process by which plants convert light, water and carbon dioxide into oxygen and the simple sugars they need to grow.

Unlike plants, mushrooms contain chitin. Although this is similar to the cellulose within the cell walls of plants, it is more commonly associated with insects and shellfish; it's found in the exoskeletons of many aquatic invertebrates.

Key terms

A mushroom is the fruiting body of fungi; all mushrooms are fungi, but not all fungi are mushrooms.

The stipe is the **stem** of the mushroom that supports the cap.

The pileus, or **cap**, is the structure on top of the mushroom with the gills or pores. The form of the cap comes in all different shapes and sizes.

Spores are microscopic single-celled reproductive units released by mushrooms once they reach maturity. They are similar to the seeds of a plant.

Hyphae are the long, branching, filamentous structures of a fungus. They're microscopic and can be fast-growing. Fungal hyphae release digestive enzymes in order to absorb nutrients from their food source.

Mycelium is the collective mass of fungal hyphae.

A **hyphal knot** is the first stage of a mushroom fruit body. The individual strands of the hyphae bundle together, forming visible bumps on the surface of the mycelium in preparation for growing a mushroom.

The **primordial** stage is usually the first glimpse of your new baby mushrooms – we call them pins, because, in some instances, they look like the heads of dressmaking pins.

The **veil** is the thin membrane that covers the underside of the cap and is linked to the stem of a young mushroom. It separates to expose the gills or pores as the mushroom grows and reaches maturity.

Spawn is a food source that forms the base on which your mushrooms will grow. Usually made from seed, grain or sawdust, it carries and feeds the mycelium network.

Substrate is a mixture of nutrient-rich organic material that the mushrooms will feed on and grow from. Different mushrooms prefer different blends of substrate mix.

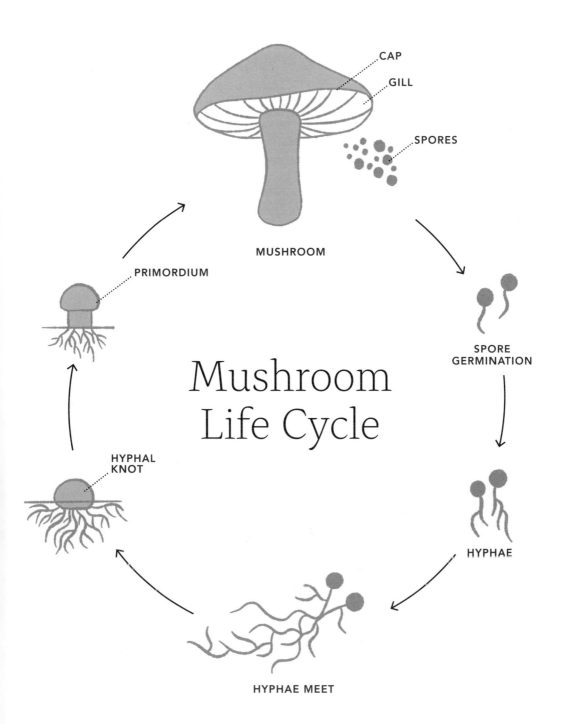

CAP

GILL

SPORES

MUSHROOM

PRIMORDIUM

SPORE
GERMINATION

Mushroom
Life Cycle

HYPHAL
KNOT

HYPHAE

HYPHAE MEET

Eating Mushrooms

Mushrooms can be consumed in a variety of ways. Fresh is the first and most obvious option, but there are only so many fresh mushrooms you can eat in a day.

Flavours

Growing your own mushrooms will open your eyes to a whole new world of flavour and texture. Most mushrooms don't travel well – they're not keen on sealed environments, plasticky surfaces or sub-zero temperatures, which is why many packaged supermarket mushrooms can quickly become damp and slimy. If you're unable to source fresh mushrooms from a local grower, cultivating your own may be the best way to sample fresh mushrooms at their finest.

Fresh mushrooms have a distinctly earthy flavour and often contain hints of familiar flavours we associate with other foods – such flavours are often used to describe their individual taste characteristics. For example, yellow oyster mushrooms have a creamy flavour similar to cashew nuts.

The richness and sometimes intensity of a mushroom's taste can be hard to pinpoint and is often described as 'umami'. The fifth of our major tastes – after sweet, sour, salty and bitter – umami is that overarching savoury sensation you experience when eating something moreish and deep in flavour.

Cooking

A perpetual supply of fresh mushrooms has helped us to hone our cooking techniques. Mushrooms contain very high levels of water that release and evaporate during the cooking process, and, as kids, we found this juice unappetising. It made our mushrooms slimy and unattractive. Today as adults, we have a more refined palate and even enjoy the juices for all their flavours and toast-soaking qualities. However, if you want to avoid losing too much water during cooking, a simple trick is to select less water-dense mushrooms, such as the yellow or pink oyster mushrooms; they crisp up nicely when fried in a little oil. Prodding and poking break down mushroom cell walls, causing them to release water. A quick fry in a shallow pan, turning half way, will leave your mushrooms a lovely golden brown and keep them firm and dry.

While we're on the subject of cell walls – we've mentioned earlier (see page 17) that mushrooms contain chitin, a fibrous compound that forms a major constituent in the exoskeletons of sea crustations and all insects, as well as mushrooms. Chitin can be hard to digest when eaten raw, and if you know someone who is intolerant to both seafood and mushrooms, there's a chance it's the chitin that is to blame. Cooking breaks down the chitin structures in the cell walls, making the mushrooms easier to digest.

Our top tips; harvest your edible mushrooms early, to prevent them drying out, and eat them straight away while they're in their prime (see pages 136–57). You can, of course, also bake or roast your mushrooms, either method will intensify their flavours.

Dried mushrooms are also a popular way of incorporating these fungi into your daily meals. The drying process intensifies their aromas and flavours (see pages 142–45) – it's what gives lion's mane its caramel undertones, and pink oyster mushrooms their essence of sweet, glazed bacon. When ground into a powder, mushrooms can be used as flavour enhancers, sauce thickeners or stocks. Try adding them to your chocolate brownie and bread mixes, or to your coffees, hot chocolates and tea infusions.

Medicinal properties

Alongside their culinary attributes, edible mushrooms are well known for their medicinal and adaptogenic qualities – adaptogens are natural substances considered to help the body cope with stress. Mushrooms have been used worldwide for centuries to cure many ailments. They are believed to help boost your immune system and brain function, reduce inflammation, fatigue and chronic metabolic conditions, and to contain antibacterial agents.

Some medicinal mushrooms are harder to consume than others. Reishi, for example, is a slow-growing and fibrous mushroom. If eaten raw it would be like chewing on a softwood stick, coupled with a very bitter taste. Reishi is best consumed as a powder or in a tincture. Powders are easily made by drying the fruits of the mushroom before grinding them finely. Other tough and woody mushrooms such as turkey tail can be processed in the same way.

You can also extract the water-soluble goodness bound up within the tougher cell walls of those that are harder to consumer by immersing them in boiling water. The boiling process not only extracts the beta-glucans compounds, but also makes it easier for our bodies to absorb the nutrients. The non-water-soluble compounds also found within many of these mushrooms can be extracted by soaking them in food-grade alcohol for 2–6 weeks.

Seasonal Growing

Mushrooms season traditionally starts in early autumn in temperate climates, when the heat of the summer subsides and the nights become cooler, and lasts until the mid-season. When coupled with frequent showers, these are the ideal conditions for mushrooms to pop. Growth then slows as the chill of the winter weather cools the deeper parts of the soil.

We say 'pop' because, despite some being slower-growing, most mushrooms that appear during this time seem to do so overnight. When a fungus is ready to fruit, all the cells it needs to grow a new mushroom are produced within a new hyphae knot. Overnight, the cells swell, drawing on the increased moisture within the environment, then divide dramatically increasing their numbers in just a few hours. Most mushroom are 80–90 per cent water, which means they can decompose as quickly as they appear.

Despite autumn being the primary season, mushrooms can be found growing year-round. Although the cold of winter traditionally slows the growth of the mycelium, it doesn't go into a state of complete dormancy; instead, it waits for temperatures to rise before preparing to fruit. During summer, when rain is sparse and the soil dry, the lack of moisture halts any spontaneous fruiting and the mycelium focuses on its own growth. Its hyphae extend cell by cell, just like a plant roots, burying deep into the soil or wood in search of nutrients.

The true morel mushroom is traditionally one of the first mushrooms kickstarts the mycelium into action. At the other end of the season, the nameko mushroom is renowned for fruiting after the first frosts or snowfall of winter, and will continue to do so until the weather begins to warm.

As in all areas of nature, there are always exceptions to the rule – a lull in the cold of winter weather or above-average spring temperatures can initiate out-of-season growth in other mushroom species. If it's been a very wet summer, mushrooms will make the most of the heat and humidity.

When considering growing in your own garden, you can source warm or cold strains of mushroom spawn, depending on when you're looking to harvest. The advantage to indoor growing is the steady ambient temperature, which is perfect for cultivating a wide variety of edible mushrooms year-round. A regular dousing of water and occasional cold shock (a few hours in the fridge) will recreate the natural conditions of the annual mushroom season.

At the Caley Brothers HQ, we run a small-scale, urban mushroom farm. We follow the seasons, opting to grows strains of mushrooms that prefer cooler temperatures during winter and strains that prefer warmer weather in summer, using electric lighting and humidity control to ensure a steady harvest. It's a low-tech, carbon-friendly approach that enables us to grow a variety of mushrooms year-round.

Basic Mushroom Care

As with anything, if you can understand the basics, the growing of all kinds of mushrooms can be easy and effective.

By growing indoors, you can cultivate a crop of mushrooms to harvest at any time of the year, whatever the weather. Indoor growth happens in short bursts; after starting up and regularly watering your grow kit, you'll see the fruits of your labour appear in only a few weeks' time. Some strains including oyster mushrooms can pop up in just one week. Other mushroom kits such as reishi and cordyceps are self-maintaining: the mushrooms grow in their own controlled environment with no watering required. A steady temperature and the right amount of light are enough for them to thrive over the course of a few months.

Outdoor growing is more labour-intensive, and the mushrooms take longer to appear. Bigger projects such as the Log Project (see page 86)

and the Morel Beds (see page 124) can take a while to incubate. The key to their success is patience and choosing the right location. With regular watering, a shaded environment and plenty of time, you should enjoy bountiful yields of mushrooms for years to come. An annual top-up of fresh spawn and substrate will also encourage continued growth.

The most common reason for the failure of mushroom kits, growing projects and inoculated logs is dehydration. As a rule of thumb, don't forget to water your mushroom projects. If your substrate feels too dry, it probably is. But before watering, remember to check to make sure it hasn't become saturated either. It's difficult to overwater your mushrooms, but it's not impossible.

Too much water on a newly laid mushroom bed can wash away the fresh spawn you've introduced, and can even drown your mycelium. A living thing, mycelium needs oxygen to thrive – if saturated this will reduce the airflow. If this happens, allow any excess water to drain away and leave your substrate to dry until it is merely damp. Don't add any more water until you're sure it's dry enough to warrant a light watering. Too much water in your substrate could also allow anaerobic bacteria to reproduce, causing your substrate to rot. In this case you might want to reconsider the position of your project; choose an area with better-draining soil or somewhere less exposed to the rain. If it's a waterlogged indoor project and has begun to smell, it might be better off in the compost heap.

Regularly inspecting your kit or peering under your woodchip is key to gauging moisture levels, making sure your mycelium is establishing itself nicely. A good sign is when you can see the mycelium beginning to coat the substrate: a clean, white, waxy layer will grow over and through the material, binding it together. Your substrate should always be damp to the touch and should smell fresh.

We have always championed the grey oyster mushroom for both indoor and outdoor growing as a beginner's best friend. It is a dominant strain that grows well, often overpowers competition from external contaminants and can be forgiving if neglected for a few days. A forgotten grey oyster mushroom grow kit can sometimes be brought back from the brink of life with an overnight soak in a bucket of water, or be preserved between growing cycles in the fridge for a couple of weeks.

What You Will Need

Darkness and stable temperatures

For indoor growing, a dark cupboard is the perfect spot for the incubation stage of growing all mushrooms. It's important you're able to keep the environment at a steady temperature – frequent fluctuations can stagnate the mycelium growth and could encourage moulds and bacteria to contaminate your substrate. You'll know if this has happened if you see green spots appear on the kit, or it develops a rancid smell. Grey oyster mushroom mycelium will often overcome many contaminants and grow in spite of them. A greater amount of spawn within your substrate is a good way to increase your chances of success, but will be unnecessary if you're able to follow and meet the growing guidelines successfully.

Grow bags

These are also known as unicorn bags, thanks to the single filter patch found at the top. Grow bags can be ordered online or from your spawn supplier and come in a variety of sizes. They are the perfect environment for incubating your substrate. The filter patch provides enough air exchange to keep your spawn alive, while keeping the risk of contamination to a minimum. Make sure you don't cover the patch during the incubation stage.

Sanitizer

A food-grade, alcohol-based sanitizer is required for sterilizing all surfaces, equipment, containers and your hands before starting any project. Always read the instructions before use.

Straw

Some straws used for pet bedding come ready treated with eucalyptus or tea tree; both have antifungal properties so will hinder any mycelium growth. Where required, therefore, always make sure you use untreated straw. Hay is not the same as straw, and we don't recommend it as a substrate for mushroom growing.

The right spawn for the job

Spawn is a simple pre-culture that is inoculated with fungi. It comes in many forms, but the type we focus on within our projects are grain and sawdust spawn, and timber dowels.

Each project will require a different type, and you will also need to consider whether you want warm- or cold-fruiting mushrooms. A few mushroom strains grow in different conditions: for example, there are warm and cold strains of lion's mane, shiitake and grey oyster. Consider using grain spawn for small indoor projects, and sawdust spawn for larger outdoor ones. Both will work for either project, although grain spawn may attract pests when used outdoors.

Your spawn may already show signs of mycelium binding the substrate particles together. You can try growing mushrooms from your pack of spawn as it stands, but there aren't masses of nutrients within your spawn mix, and we want you to grow as large a crop as possible. That's why we encourage you to add your spawn to other forms of substrate – this feeds your spawn, encouraging more mushrooms to fruit.

The bigger the project and the firmer your chosen substrate, the longer it can take for your spawn to colonize: for example, 1kg (2¼lb) coffee kit can be fully colonized and ready to grow in just twenty-one days, whereas a thick chunk of freshly felled hardwood could take 9–24 months. You will get many more mushrooms from your log over the course of a few years compared to your coffee kit, which will fruit for only a few months before it's spent and ready for the compost heap.

Fresh spawn is key to successful growing. Always use a reputable, dedicated supplier – which should provide you with spawn that is perfect for your project. Make sure you keep your spawn according to your supplier's instructions and use it within the recommended time frame – your supplier can advise you of this before you place your order.

The correct way to store spawn can vary depending on the strain and supplier guidelines. But, more often than not, it should be kept in the fridge until you're ready to use it. Beware that not all strains like to be chilled at low temperatures, or for too long, while some can be stored in near-freezing conditions for a few months.

Wood

For a number of our outdoor projects, we specify freshly felled wood. The reason is to ensure that no other fungus has had a chance to inoculate your wood and that it hasn't dried out. For best results, always use hardwood or fruit-tree wood. Contact your spawn supplier to make sure you purchase the best spawn for the type of wood that you have access to.

Our Five Tips for Success

Make sure your hands, work surfaces and equipment are clean

Mould is potentially the biggest threat to your mushroom-growing projects. Therefore, before starting any grow project, we always advise you to wash and sterilize your work surfaces and equipment.

When growing mushrooms or embarking on the inoculation stage of any growing, your objective is to create the best environment for your mycelium to thrive. Unlucky for us, these conditions are also ideal for bacteria and other fungi, including moulds. So clean hands and equipment are the best way to keep the intruders at bay.

Order your spawn and grow kits from reputable suppliers

Fresh is best, and sometimes the only way you can guarantee this is to go straight to a local, reputable supplier. Your new mushroom passion will also be their long-term mushroom passion, and giving you the best product to ensure your growing success is very much in their interest.

Don't mix your spawn types

You might love the idea of your grow kits or logs growing two different types of mushrooms. However, if you mix your spawns or inoculated dowels, one species will always dominate the weaker. The success rate of the dominant spawn will be reduced, and the potential of the less dominant mushroom strain eradicated. You run the risk that neither survives.

Keep your project out of direct sunlight and well hydrated

In the wild, mushrooms are often found in shaded, humid environments. When growing your own mushrooms, you're looking to replicate these conditions indoors (by spraying your grow kit and keeping it out of direct sunlight) or outdoors (with regular watering). The sun will dry any growing project or new mushrooms, reducing your chances of growing success.

Good airflow at every stage

Maintaining a good circulation of fresh air is important to the success of many mushroom grow projects. Like us, mushrooms absorb oxygen and expire carbon dioxide, even during the incubation stage, which is why we use specific grow bags for our smaller projects. The filter patch allows the mycelium to breath. During the growing process, oxygen levels can alter the form of your mushrooms. If the air is stagnant, a build-up of CO_2 can cause the caps of oyster mushrooms to be smaller and the stems longer. Too much air can make a difference, too; when lion's mane mushrooms are grown in a draught, they'll change colour, turning brown and drying out.

Sometimes altering the environment deliberately can lead to fascinating results, like the sculptural antlers of reishi grow kits.

Harvesting

For us, every stage of growing mushrooms is the best stage. The anticipation as you prepare them to grow; the watching and waiting and watching some more; and that rush of excitement when you notice that your first mushrooms are on the cusp of fruiting.

We have been growing mushrooms for many years now, but the harvesting stage still fills our hearts with pride – in a way that only nurturing something as it grows does. You can be happy in the knowledge that what you're growing is not only stunning (regardless of its form) but also delicious.

We get asked lots of questions about when and how to harvest mushrooms. Each will be slightly different, and there is a wealth of knowledge and guidance within your purchased grow kit and project instructions, as well as in guidebooks and online.

The first and most important step is to correctly assess any mushroom that you're planning to harvest. To correctly identify a mushroom, you must assess: its habitat; its overall appearance, including the stem, cap, gills and veil; its spore prints; and its internal flesh. Then, when you are completely certain as to the identity, use your hands or a sharp blade to remove the mushrooms as close to the base as possible.

Under no circumstances should you consume any mushrooms unless you are 100 per cent sure you know what they are.

When to harvest

A sure sign that a mushroom has reached maturity is when its gills or pores become exposed, and they start to drop their spores. Mushrooms release a proliferation of spores after they've reached maturity. You may notice a covering of these around the base of your indoor grow kit once your mushrooms are ready to harvest. The spore dusting under your kit can be wiped away with a damp cloth.

INDOOR GROWING
As a rule, you should harvest all the fruiting bodies at once. It is not often that you are able to pick some of the larger mushrooms and allow the rest to continue growing. If left unharvested, any remaining mushrooms will begin to dry out and wither.

The exceptions to this rule are cremini and button mushrooms. These will fruit sporadically, allowing you to harvest them individually as they reach the desired size.

After harvesting, leave the substrate to rest for a while. This will allow the mycelium to recover and prepare for a second harvest.

OUTDOOR GROWING

Outdoors, your mushrooms will continue to sporadically fruit and it's best to harvest these as and when they appear. A slightly earlier harvest is recommended as your garden's minibeasts will also be looking to dine out on your fresh crop of delicious mushrooms – make sure to get there first.

How to harvest

Pinch or slice your mushrooms at their base using a sharp knife or a pair of scissors; try not to rip the mycelium from its substrate.

INDOOR GROWING

Take the mushroom stem right back to the base when removing the whole cluster or fruiting body, to prevent contamination and your project from spoiling.

OUTDOOR GROWING

When harvesting outdoors, whether a home project or from a lesser-known source, always ensure you're harvesting safe and edible mushrooms, because outdoor growing will always carry a high risk of contamination from wild spores.

Storing

Freshly harvested mushrooms will keep well in the fridge for a few days. They're best stored in a paper bag or left unwrapped on a piece of kitchen tissue. If kept in a sealed container, they'll sweat and deteriorate quickly. To prolong the edible quality of your mushrooms you might consider drying them (see page 142).

Spent Substrate

Mushroom substrate is a mix of organic materials and fresh mushroom spawn. When left to incubate the spawn within the substrate develops into mycelium. In the right conditions, the substrate will produce a wonderful mushroom crop.

Spent substrate is a natural by-product of any mushroom farm, and a by-product of yours if you've been growing your own. Once the last of your mushrooms have been harvested and the nutrients depleted, what remains is a substrate still teeming with living mycelium eager to find more nutrients to flourish again. Such spent mushroom substrate – or what we here at the Caley Brothers HQ like to call 'gardeners' gold' – can do wonderful things for your soil and garden. We actively promote putting your used substrate into your compost, burying it in your garden or crumbling it onto your pot plants. (See pages 112, 116 and 128.)

A healthy amount of mycelium is key to good soil health. The mycelium within your soil and the plants in your garden can develop a symbiotic relationship when combined, exchanging nutrients so that both fungi and plants can thrive (see pages 108 and 116). Mycelium is a natural decomposer, breaking down any waste material or leaf mulch left on the top layer of your soil. In digesting the detritus, it absorbs the nutrients it needs and then converts them into digestible nutrients for surrounding plants – but not before producing a last crop of mushrooms if the circumstances are just right.

Mycelium is known to penetrate deep into the soil – often aided by worms, which draw it down, aerating the soil as they go – thereby extending the reach of most of your garden plants' roots. It draws on deep water reserves during the drier months and supports plant growth with vitamins and nutrients that would otherwise be out of reach.

We are mushroom farmers, and so not very well versed in gardening practices. However, taking into account what we have discovered regarding the mycelium network – we openly advocate for the no-dig approach to gardening. The tilling process shreds the mycelium network in your topsoil, loosening the soil and increasing the risk of erosion. Mycelium is often described as the egg in the cake mix, the binder that holds all the key ingredients together. This action also locks in huge quantities of carbon, so each time we turn the soil the bonds are broken and carbon is released back into the atmosphere. Mycelium is quick to recover, but not before much damage has been done.

Foraging

The growing process is hugely therapeutic. As siblings, we came together to grow mushrooms to improve our diet, but it soon became bigger than that.

We came to appreciate the process as a connection to nature, and for all the benefits it brings. From that grew a commitment to spend more time in nature, even if only for thirty minutes a day. We have since lost ourselves for hours in woodlands, captivated by the mushrooms we would spot near our homes, among the undergrowth and on the sides of trees.

Mushroom spotting is now second nature to us, and we do it whenever we're outdoors. Once you start looking, you soon realize mushrooms grow everywhere – not just in the woods! Shaggy inkcap mushrooms like recently disturbed soil and can be found at the edges of car parks and tracks in urban settings; puffballs love a close-cut sports lawn; chicken of the woods will grow on fruit trees lining an urban street; and King Alfred's cake can be found growing at the base of a mature beech (*Fagus*) tree year-round.

Of course, this book is primarily about growing your own, but we encourage you to get outdoors and discover the wonderful world of wild mushrooms too. In this section we provide some pointers and tips for starting your mushroom-spotting journey – the perfect way to while away the hours as you're waiting for your project to incubate.

There are many identifiable forms of fruiting fungi beyond the toadstool, including lichens and bracket fungi. Of the 15,000 types of wild fungi that exist in the UK, all can be categorized very broadly into three groups.

Mycorrhizal fungi

It is said that nearly all plant life on earth benefits from a relationship with these fungi, as they have a symbiotic relationship with plants, and some species of mycorrhizal fungi develop unique relationships with specific species of tree. Such trees can become landmarks, guiding well-versed foragers to the presence of certain types of mushrooms.

Unlike plants, mushrooms don't make their own food; instead, they seek it out and digest it. By establishing a strong, and nurturing symbiotic relationship with plants, mushrooms can exchange nutrients and minerals in return for glucose. It is this special relationship that almost entirely inhibits the purposeful cultivation of a few well-desired mushrooms, such as truffles and chanterelles.

Saprotrophs

Oyster, shiitake, cremini and portobello mushrooms are typical saprotrophs, which live and feed on dead and dying organic matter. By releasing digestive enzymes, they break down surrounding decaying matter. Their hyphae (essentially their 'roots') then absorb many of the nutrients needed while the rest are turned back into nutrient-rich food for the surrounding vegetation. It's easy to recreate many of the environments in which this type of mushrooms grows.

Parasitic fungi

When the spores of parasitic fungi land on a host, they release enzymes that, over time, completely infect that host. These fungi, in turn, become saprotrophs. Not all parasitic fungi are limited to plants including trees. Cordyceps is a type of parasitic fungi that grow on specific insects and have the unusual ability to control the movements of its host body; they can direct the host to the best position for the fungi to fruit and disperse spores.

We need to talk about false and poisonous mushrooms

In the world it's estimated that there are 2.3–3.8 million types of fungi. Some 15,000 have been identified within the UK, 300 of which are edible, and some of the inedible ones look very similar to their edible counterparts. These often have the word 'false' attached to their common name by way of identification, such as the false morel (*Gyromitra* sp.) or the false chanterelle (*Hygrophoropsis aurantiaca*). Others have appropriately descriptive names to ensure they're given a wide berth, including the death cap, deadly webcap, destroying angel and the funeral bell.

We highly recommend using a combination of apps and guidebooks to get familiar with the more easily identifiable mushrooms that have no lookalikes. Naturally there will be some variations and similarities in the fruiting bodies of mushrooms that make them difficult to identify from a single image in a guidebook. The accurate form of identification is through a microscope and genetic analysis, but, of course, these aren't always to hand. In some parts of Europe, where foraging is a part of everyday life, you can take wild mushrooms into pharmacies and have them identified on the spot. Unfortunately, here in the UK there is no such service, so we have to rely on other forms of identification. This is why it is so important not to eat anything if you are in any doubt over its identity.

Foraging rules

When picking any mushrooms, here are a few foraging rules that we like to endorse:

- If you find a bountiful supply of mushrooms, do not take any more than you need. Always leave some for nature, or one day there may be no more left to pick.

- Collect your mushrooms in a wicker or woven basket. When you forage you too become part of the ecosystem; the spores from the mushrooms you have picked will fall through the gaps in the wicker weave and continue to spread among the forest during your foray.

- Not all edible mushrooms are for harvesting. Some are still rare and protected under Section 8 of the Wildlife and Countryside Act 1998, making them illegal to pick. One of these is the lion's mane mushroom: you can look, but please don't touch.

- When harvesting, detach the fruiting bodies with a knife, or pull them away close to their base. Using a knife will mean you take less dirt away with your mushrooms.

- Always pick from a safe space that is not hazardous to reach, and where the mushrooms are well away from passing dogs and busy roads.

- Always cook outdoor harvested mushrooms before eating them.

Under Harvesting (see pages 32–3) we talk about the key considerations in correctly identifying mushrooms. These apply both when growing at home or when harvesting from the wild. Remember the wise words of Terry Pratchett – 'all fungi are edible, some fungi are only edible once'.

Troubleshooting

There are a few common problems you are likely to encounter when growing your own mushrooms.

Flies

Tiny black flies are a common visitor to indoor mushroom-growing projects (if you own houseplants, you'll know the ones we mean). In this case, they're likely a fungus fly, and are relatively harmless. That said, they will thrive inside mushroom substrate if left unattended. Therefore, it's best to finish harvesting any mushrooms and move your substrate on to the compost heap.

Green moulds

Trichoderma is a very common green-coloured filamentous fungus that has a similar appearance to the mould you see growing on a loaf of bread. It can appear anywhere on your substrate during the incubation or fruiting stages. It likes warm temperatures so is more common during summer. Many mushrooms, especially on a first flush, will power through a small spot or two of *trichoderma*, and grow despite it. To avoid the mould, you can open your grow kit in a different area to the mould spot. If a larger area has been contaminated, and it's difficult to avoid when opening your kit, your mushrooms are unlikely to grow, and you're probably best assigning them to the compost heap.

Mushrooms are growing too soon, or in the wrong place

Mushrooms wait for no one, and there's always a chance your mushrooms could fruit when you least expect it – it's the way of nature. As soon as you notice your eager mushrooms pop, take them out of where you have them stored and give them a good dousing of water to help them hydrate. If they're growing in an unexpected area, you can help them flourish by giving them the room they need to develop. This may involve opening your grow kit a little wider or reorientating its position to help them thrive.

Should your mushrooms have grown excessively in the wrong place – for example, squashed together inside your grow bag – don't worry, you can still salvage your kit. Harvest the deformed crop and compost. Then rest your kit and repeat the growing instruction to achieve another flush.

No mushrooms

There are many reasons mushrooms don't grow, one of the biggest being that the environment isn't quite right for them to fruit. Go back and read the instructions for your grow kit again, to make sure you have set up the very best conditions for your grow project. Is there a chance your spawn could have been inhibited during its storage time, or during the incubation period? Occasionally mushrooms just need more time.

If no mushrooms have appeared in the expected time frame, check to see whether your mycelium and substrate are looking bright and healthy; they should be neither too dry or too damp, and should smell fresh and earthy. See also the cold-shock method on page 24.

Rancid smells

Every stage of the mushroom-growing process should smell fresh and mushroomy. Your sense of smell is the best tool for assessing the freshness of your spawn, mycelium, substrate and mushrooms. Hints of vinegar, bad feet, sour or even fishy odours are a sign of bacterial build-up within your spawn or substrate, which will compromise growth. Check regularly for changes to your substrate and dispose of anything that doesn't smell fresh into your compost.

Spawn clumping

Your fresh spawn will need to be kept cool, to help preserve it. During this time, the mycelium will carry on growing, and you could find that it's bonded the spawn together into large clumps, making for uneven distribution throughout your substrate. You can easily break the spawn back down so it's loose, by squeezing it and rubbing it between your fingers. There's no need to take your spawn out of its protective bag, either; gently press the bag as you would a bag of precooked rice. This will keep the spawn clean and reduce any risk of contamination. Should you need to use your hands directly, make sure they are clean and sanitized, along with any other equipment you use. Always refer to the storage instructions from your spawn provider for the best way to store your fresh spawn.

Yellow liquids

An excess of liquid on the surface of your mycelium is a waste product of mycelium. A small amount of pale liquid is a common part of the growing process. However, a large quantity of darker-coloured secretions suggests your mycelium could be battling with a contaminant. When you open your grow kit, the excess liquid will drain away. If your kit has become completely contaminated, it will develop a rancid smell.

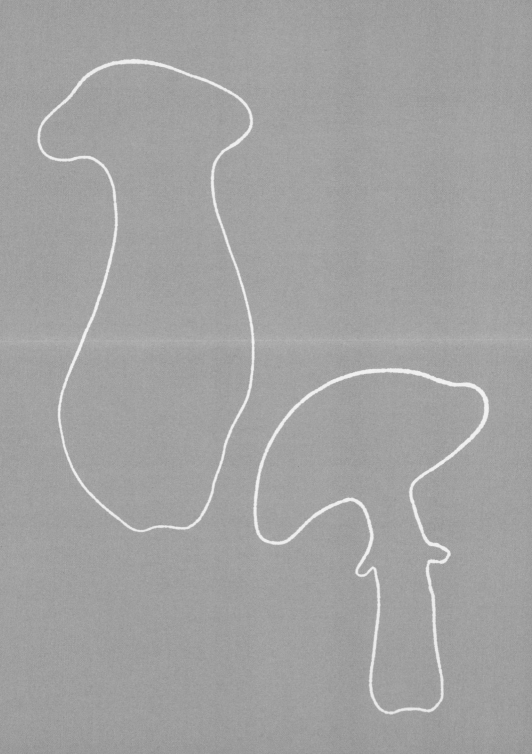

Part 2
Mushroom Projects

Caffeine Hit
Grow mushrooms on your used coffee grounds

Oyster mushrooms love and thrive on the nutrients in used coffee grounds. Collect your own or ask your local coffee shop to give you theirs (they'll have plenty!). Espresso grounds are best for growing mushrooms, as the coffee-making process means your substrate is already pasteurized, hydrated and ready to grow.

WHEN Year-round.

WHERE You will need to leave your kit to colonize for 21 days in the dark at a constant temperature of 17–20°C (63–68°F). Once incubated and ready to grow, place in a bright spot where you will remember to water it and be able to watch it grow – next to the kitchen sink or on a windowsill are both good options.

Method

Getting started
If collecting your own used coffee grounds, freeze immediately after brewing, breaking up any large lumps with a clean spoon first, and so gradually build up to the quantity needed. The freezing process helps preserve the coffee and reduces the chance of contamination. If collecting from a coffee house, the coffee must have been freshly brewed the day you plan to make your project. If you're unable to set up your project immediately, be sure to freeze the coffee grounds on the day you collect them.

When you have the quantity required, take your coffee grounds out of the freezer and leave to defrost for 6–8 hours. Remove your spawn from the fridge once your grounds have defrosted and allow it to reach room temperature. Remember to use your gloves and sanitize your hands, utensils and work surfaces before getting started to reduce the risk of contamination and to give your mushrooms the best chance of success.

MUSHROOMS

Grey oyster (*Pleurotus ostreatus*)
Italian oyster (*Pleurotus pulmonarius*)
Pearl oyster (*Pleurotus ostreatus*)
Pink oyster (*Pleurotus djamor*)
White oyster (*Pleurotus cornucopiae*)

MATERIALS
• Used coffee grounds, max. weight 1kg (2¼lb). (Grounds collected from a cafetiere are not recommended as they'll contain too much water.)
• Fresh, oyster-mushroom-grain spawn 100g (3½oz)*
• Pair of clean rubber gloves
• Alcohol spray or sanitizer
• Small mushroom growbag, 10.5 × 35.5 × 6.5cm (4 × 14 × 2¾in), with filter
• Self-adhesive label or tape
• Lidded container
• Pen
• Pair of clean scissors
• Mister/spray bottle

* For best results, aim for a 10–12 per cent ratio of spawn to coffee-grounds substrate.

Once ready, break down any lumps of spawn and mix them in with your coffee grounds until evenly distributed. Carefully place the coffee and spawn mixture into the growbag, making sure not to fill above the filter patch. Try not to press down as you go; you want air to be able to circulate through the mixture.

Leave a sizable gap of at least 6cm (2½in) above the top of the mixture for air exchange. Then seal the growbag at the top by folding it over a couple of times and securing with the label or tape, again making sure you haven't covered the filter patch, which allows the mycelium to breathe.

Place the growbag in a dark location with a steady temperature between 17–20°C (63–38°F), making sure the temperature doesn't fluctuate. A kitchen cupboard is usually a good spot. During this time your coffee will become completely colonized with the mushroom spawn, turning white as the mycelium begins

to consume the nutrients in the coffee and bind all the ingredients together. Your bag will soon become firm to hold.

Growing your mushrooms

After twenty-one days, remove your growbag from storage. With scissors, cut a 12cm (5in) 'X' shape in the front of the growbag. Then fold its top over and refix, so that this time you are covering up the filter patch and removing the air pocket at the top of the bag. By reducing this space, you will encourage growth from the front of your growbag.

Spray the opening of your kit twice a day, and more regularly during warmer weather, above 22°C (72°F). This keeps the opening humid and will signal to the mushrooms that it is time to grow. After 7–14 days of daily spraying, you should see your primordial growth appear – keep them hydrated with twice daily spraying.

Your mushroom pins (primordia) will double in size over the next 12–24 hours and will continue to do so until they're fully grown, in about 5–7 days (note that mushrooms develop more slowly in cooler temperatures).

Harvesting your mushrooms
The best time to pick or harvest your mushrooms is when the caps begin to flatten out. Hold the cluster firmly in your hand, pinch close to the base and gently twist. The mushrooms will tear away from the substrate block easily. Make sure you harvest all your mushrooms at the same time, regardless of their size.

TIP After harvesting your first mushrooms, reseal the growbag and leave the substrate to rest in somewhere dark. After ten days, submerge your growbag in clean cold water overnight, to rehydrate the kit and initiate a second flush. Keep your kit moist and watch out for signs of contamination which will inhibit new growth. Contaminated lumps can be removed with a clean spoon.

Make Your Own Spawn

Grow spawn at home using the stem-butt method

This is one of our simpler projects and it takes you back to the basics, providing a window to the mycelium-growing process and a close-up look at how mushrooms can resurrect themselves. Once the substrate – in this case cardboard – is colonized, you can transfer your home-grown spawn onto another growing project.

There is some risk of contamination from the mushrooms or the cardboard, but it's still worth having a go. You should see the mycelium developing in as little as ten days and could be harvesting more mushrooms within six weeks.

We have recommended grey oyster mushrooms for this project as they are fast-growing and readily available.

WHEN You can do this project at any time of the year. The warmer the ambient temperature, the quicker the substrate will become fully colonized. Cool indoor temperatures will slow down the growth of mycelium.

WHERE This is the perfect indoor project. Store your substrate in a dark cupboard, ideally at a steady temperature of 16–20°C (61–68°F).

MUSHROOMS

Grey oyster (*Pleurotus ostreatus*)

MATERIALS

• Alcohol sanitizer wipes or spray

• 2 pieces of ink- and tape-free plain cardboard, approx. 40 × 40cm (16 × 16in)

• 2 plastic containers (with lids) approx. 20 × 10 × 8cm (8 × 4 × 3¼in)

• Boiling water – enough to half-fill your plastic container, covering all the cardboard

• Hand drill

• 3mm (1/8in) drill bit

• 50g (2oz) fresh, grey oyster mushroom stems, roughly chopped into 1cm (½in) pieces and kept refrigerated until needed

Method

Getting started

This method is low-tech, so you need to reduce the risk of contamination by keeping work surfaces, containers and your hands clean and using alcohol wipes or spray.

Tear your cardboard into small pieces of 3x3cm (1¼ x 1¼in) each. Place the pieces into your first container and carefully cover with boiling water. Put the lid on the container and leave it to cool to room temperature. This may take a couple of hours.

Once cool, drain the water. With clean hands, press any excess water out of the cardboard – it should be wet but not soaking.

Prepare your second container by drilling two holes, spaced 5cm (2in) apart, in each side of the container – this is to allow air exchange during the spawn run. Then clean this container thoroughly with your sanitizer wipes.

Insert layers of your chopped mushroom stems and cardboard pieces in the container, making sure there's a good mix and even distribution of stems and cardboard. Do not compact them together.

Incubation

Keep your container in the dark at a stable temperature. If the temperature fluctuates too much at this stage, there is a risk of contamination. A kitchen cupboard is a good option – choose somewhere you'll remember to check in on.

After ten days, check your container. You should notice that the cardboard is turning white – this is a healthy covering of mycelium. It may take as long as twenty-one days to become completely colonized. Check your container every few days.

Once fully colonized (covered in a layer of white, fluffy mycelium), you have your very own mushroom spawn. This can be transferred to a new substrate and used to grow fresh, home-grown mushrooms.

TIP Projects in which you can use your new spawn include: Caffeine Hit (see page 44); Greenhouse or Polytunnel Growing (see page100); and Grow a Mushroom Book (see page 64).

Hanging Mycelium Ornaments

Plastic-free crafting ideas

Mycelium is the vegetive body of the mushroom, and it binds together the substrate it is grown from. In this project we make the most of this natural process to create hanging ornaments that can be grown and dried before being decorated for display.

Together with everyday household objects, we've adapted the simple process used to make mushroom-based packaging and products. With care and attention, your ornaments can last for many years, and once finished with can be composted.

WHEN All through the year; the crafting process takes about a week to complete.

WHERE In the kitchen, at a table or on a workbench.

MUSHROOMS

Grey oyster (*Pleurotus ostreatus*)
Reishi (*Ganoderma lingzhi*)

MATERIALS

(for four large ornaments)

• 4 large cookie cutters, approx. 8cm (3¼in) tall
• Alcohol spray
• Bowl
• 300g (10oz) hardwood pellets
• 450ml (16fl. oz) water
• String, 80cm (32in) long
• Scissors
• Protective rubber gloves
• 25ml (1fl. oz) thin bleach (not thick bleach)
• 50g (2oz) flour
• 250g (9oz) grey oyster or reishi spawn on sawdust or grain
• Large bowl
• Baking paper
• Baking tray
• Growbag large enough to fit the baking tray
• Sticky tape

Method

Getting started

Ensure you have clean hands and work surfaces. Sterilize your cookie cutters with your alcohol spray and leave to dry.

In a bowl, rehydrate the hardwood pellets in the water; this will take approximately 30 minutes.

In the meantime, take your string and with the scissors, cut it into four equal lengths. Using gloves, soak the string pieces in the bleach for two minutes. Remove and set aside in a safe spot.

Once the hardwood pellets have absorbed all the water, mix in the flour and the spawn, to create a mycelium mix.

Creating your ornaments

Place the baking paper flat on a worktop or table and lay the cookie cutters on top: this creates a clean surface to work from. Loop each piece of string through each of your cookie cutters; this way your string will become secured in place as the mycelium grows and takes holds within the shape of the cookie cutter. Then completely fill your cookie cutter with the mycelium mixture, covering the ends of the string and knot. Make sure you press the filling down as you go so its compacted.

Place your filled cookie cutters into your growbag, making sure they lie flat on the baking tray and are not sitting on top of each other. Seal the bag by folding the end over a couple of times and securing with the tape. Place the bag (with the cutters) on a flat surface in a dark place.

Incubating stage

Gradually, you will see white mycelial growth beginning to cover your substrate mix. After seven days, your shapes will feel firm to the touch and should be completely covered in white mycelium. Remove the cookie cutters from the growbag and with clean hands and on a clean surface gently press the shapes out of the cutters.

Carefully place your mycelium shapes back in the growbag and leave in the dark for a further three days. This is to ensure the mycelium continues to grow over every surface of your shapes. Then remove your shapes from the bag and place on a clean sheet of baking paper on a clean baking tray. Preheat your oven to 140°C (275°F/gas mark 1), and once at the correct temperature, place the baking tray with the ornaments in the oven and bake for 45 minutes. Remove from the oven and leave to cool. Once your decorations are completely cold, they are ready to hang or decorate.

TIP You could consider painting your decorations or finishing with a decoupage or gold-leaf effect. If looked after, your decorations will last a couple of years. Once they're no longer needed, they can be composted and will decompose in a matter of weeks.

Mushroom Paper

Making your own paper textiles from foraged mushrooms

Some of the slower-growing and more woody mushrooms growing on decaying trees can be harvested and used for making paper. Polypore mushrooms are particularly good for this as the fibres are similar to the wood pulp that paper is made from. The cell walls of mushrooms contain chitin, which can also be found in the exoskeletons of lobsters, shrimp and insects, and is similar to the cellulose in trees and other plants.

In this project we break down the tough mushroom material and turn it into a pulp before transforming it into beautiful artisan paper. Diverse mushrooms will produce different-coloured paper. This method creates around four sheets of paper.

WHEN Bracket fungi may be found in woodland throughout the year.

WHERE Perfect for the kitchen.

MUSHROOMS

Birch polypore (*Fomitopsis betulina*)

Turkey tail (*Trametes versicolor*)

MATERIALS

- 2.6 litres (4½ pints) water
- 120g (4oz) dried mushrooms or 500g (1lb 1½oz) of fresh – either foraged or sourced online or from a wholefood store
- Wide shallow bowl, big enough to place your splatter screen inside
- Food processor or blender
- Roasting tin
- Wire mesh splatter screen
- Clean towels
- Large dry sponge
- Rolling pin/heavy book (optional)

Method

Getting started

Boil your water and use it to rehydrate your dry mushrooms by submerging them in the boiled water in the bowl until they soften; this should take around 30 minutes.

Add half of your soaked mushrooms and water into your food processor and blend to a pulp. You may need to add extra cold water – you're aiming for a loose mixture similar to that of a potato soup. Pour the mushroom pulp into your roasting tin and repeat for the rest of the mushrooms and water.

Slide your mesh splatter screen into the roasting tin making sure it is immersed under the mushroom pulp. Slowly raise the screen while gently swishing it from side to side so that the mushroom pulp settles on the mesh in an even layer. It will be quite thick at this point. You can tap the screen to allow some of the water to drain out.

Carefully place a towel over the top of your screen and turn the screen over. Lie the towel flat on a table with the mushroom pulp and screen on top. Use the sponge to gently press the top of your screen, pushing the mixture away from the screen and on to the towel. The towel and sponge will absorb much of the moisture.

Use a separate dry towel to press the screen down on to your mushroom pulp and achieve your desired paper thickness. Any thin spots can be patched with more mushroom pulp. Lift the screen to reveal your layer of damp mushroom 'paper'. Repeat this process until most of the pulp has gone from the slurry mix. You should come away with around four sheets of 'paper'.

Leave your 'paper' sheets to partially dry on the towels for about 36 hours. If you like, you can gently press the paper with a rolling pin during the drying stage, to create a more even texture. If your paper starts to curl and wrinkle as it dries, flatten it by lying a heavy weight such as a book on top for a day or two.

The paper sheets will take around three days to fully dry. Once dry, you can slice your mushroom sheets into rectangles, or leave them as they are for a more artisan effect.

TIP If you want to try this project with shop-bought mushrooms; you can include some soaked recycled paper in your slurry mix. This can be added at the very beginning, and blended alongside your mushrooms, you need only enough to make the mushroom pulp consistency.

Mushroom Ink
Getting creative with inkcaps

Mushrooms from the inkcap genus *Coprinopsis* are well known for their rapid deterioration on reaching maturity or once picked. They beautifully melt away to disperse their spores. This process (deliquesce) turns the mushroom into a sludgy black liquid and it's this earthy, dark sepia-coloured liquid that we're going to make into a usable ink. Historically, common inkcaps have been harvested to make ink for important documents.

Mica inkcaps grow in smaller clumps than common ones; when mature, they begin to turn black at the edges. Shaggy mane mushrooms are particularly good for this project as they grow in clusters, meaning they are easier to spot when foraging.

WHEN When inkcaps are in season, from mid-spring to mid-autumn. They like to grow in grassy meadows and also on disturbed land, so you might find them around edges of car parks or urban green spaces.

WHERE The kitchen.

Method

Getting started
Clean your container by spraying with sanitizer and wiping dry. Then place your mushrooms into the container and store in the fridge for a week. They will begin to decompose after just twelve hours. You can speed up the decomposition process by leaving your mushrooms out of the fridge for a few days.

Once duly decomposed, blend your mushrooms into a loose pulp/inky liquid. Strain the liquid through your muslin cloth into the saucepan and discard the remaining mushroom pulp.

Bring to the boil and simmer for about four minutes. With a wooden spoon, stir in a couple of drops of your chosen essential oil, to remove the pungent mushroom smell and to help preserve the ink. Decant the ink into your sterilized glass jar and screw the lid on tight. Store in the fridge.

MUSHROOMS *
Mica inkcap (*Coprinellus micaceus*)
Shaggy mane (*Coprinus comatus*)
Common inkcaps (*Coprinopsis atramentaria*)

MATERIALS
- Tupperware or plastic container with a lid
- Sanitizer/alcohol spray
- Clean cloth
- 6–8 mature, large mushrooms
- Food blender
- Muslin cloth
- Saucepan
- Wooden spoon
- Essential oil such as tea tree or eucalyptus oil, a few drops
- Sterilized glass jar with lid

* WARNING: common inkcaps are poisonous if consumed, so be careful.

TIP Although shaggy mane mushrooms are considered edible and regarded as delicious when eaten soon after picking, they have highly toxic effects when consumed with alcohol.

Grow a Mushroom Book

Accessorize your home with decorative oyster mushrooms

This creative indoor project demonstrates how a mycelium network can suffuse simple substrates such as books, binding the pages together before producing a crop of stunning mushrooms in just a few weeks.

WHEN This indoor project can be made year-round.

WHERE Once started, you need to leave your project to inoculate for 21 days in the dark, at a constant temperature of 17–20°C (63–68°F). You should place your inoculated book in a bright spot, one in clear view, so that you remember to water it and can watch it grow. Next to the kitchen sink or on a shaded windowsill are good options.

Method

Getting started

Wash and dry your hands, and sanitize the work surfaces and equipment to reduce the risk of contamination.

Place your book in the heatproof container and cover it with boiling water. Ensure you submerge the whole book, using a wooden spoon or tongs to press the book below the surface of the water. Leave to cool.

Remove your bag of spawn from the fridge and allow it to reach room temperature. Give the contents of the bag a squeeze to break up the spawn, while keeping the bag sealed.

Once your book is cool enough to handle, empty the excess water from the container, and allow the book to drain for a few minutes. Then carefully open the book and check to make sure the water has soaked through most of the pages. Be gentle as the spine of the book could now be fragile.

Take your bag of broken-up spawn and sprinkle it in sections among the pages. Once all the spawn is distributed throughout the book, close and place it into the growbag with the filter patch. Press down on the book so that the spawn is firmly compressed and the book lies flat. Seal the growbag by

MUSHROOMS

Grey oyster (*Pleurotus ostreatus*)
Pink oyster (*Pleurotus djamor*)
Yellow oyster (*Pleurotus citrinopileatus*)

MATERIALS

• Heatproof container large enough to submerge your book
• Book, approx. 13 × 20 × 2.5cm (5 × 8 × 1in), with fewer than 400 pages and printed within the last 10 years; this will ensure your book has been printed with lead-free, soy-based ink, so your mushrooms will be safe and delicious to eat
• Boiling water
• Wooden spoon or tongs
• 75g (3oz) grey oyster mushroom grain spawn; kept refrigerated until needed. If growing yellow or pink oyster mushrooms, increase the spawn amount to 100g (4oz) and check storage instructions for spawn storage with your supplier.
• Mushroom growbag, 25 × 50cm (10 × 20in), with filter patch
• Sticky tape, to seal your growbag
• Mister/spray bottle

folding the top over a couple of times and taping it in place. Be careful not to cover the white filter patch – spawn is a living organism and needs a good supply of oxygen to thrive.

Place your growbag in a dark location at a temperature of 17–20°C (63–68°F) for up to 21 days, until the book is fully ready. You will know when it's colonized as there will be a good layer of white fuzz covering the pages and bonding them together. This is the mycelium from the spawn consuming the paper of your book.

To initiate fruiting

Remove the cover of your book. Once the pages are covered in a layer of white mycelium, to help initiate fruiting, you should introduce light, oxygen and humidity to your book by removing it from its growbag. Then sit it on a clean plate or other surface and move it into a light airy spot, where you will remember to spray it with water twice a day (or more regularly in warmer weather). A good amount of light and water throughout the day will initiate primordial growth. Once the little pins (primordia) begin to show, your mushrooms will grow rapidly over the following 5–7 days.

When your oyster mushrooms start to fruit, keep spraying them twice a day, to avoid them drying out.

Harvesting your mushrooms

Your mushrooms should be ready to harvest 5–7 days after they first appear. Do this when their caps start flattening out.

To remove the mushrooms, pinch and twist close to the base of each cluster. Store your oyster mushrooms in a paper bag in the fridge until you're ready to eat them.

There is not much nutrition in a book, so you are likely to only get one harvest of mushrooms from this project.

TIP Grey oyster mushrooms are incredibly resilient and a great beginner mushroom to experiment with. Once mastered, this project is well worth trying with yellow and pink oyster mushroom spawn. They're stunning to watch grow as well as delicious to eat.

Mushroom Macramé

Like it or knot – mushrooms for display

What we love about this macramé-and-mushroom project is its simple but stunning results.

Fresh, home-grown mushrooms are glorious and wonderful to watch flourishing, but sometimes the kits themselves are not so special to look at. Here we encourage you to embrace the wonderful craft of macramé as a way of glamourizing your kit and the growing process. A knotted plant hanger is perfect for displaying your own home-grown mushrooms, combining beauty with a practical twist.

WHEN This project can be made with almost any indoor mushroom grow kit, year-round.

WHERE At home, in your greenhouse or in the workspace. The location should receive plenty of natural light, but be sure to keep your macramé out of direct sunlight.

MUSHROOMS

Any grow-at-home kits that fit within your macramé.

MATERIALS

- Grow-at-home mushroom kit
- Macramé hanger
- Pen
- Scissors

Method

Getting started

Follow the preparation instructions for your grow-at-home mushroom kit.

Once you reach the point where you need to make openings for the mushrooms to grow through hold off and first place your kit inside your macramé hanger. Then choose and mark the best positions for the openings, before removing your kit from the hanger and creating the appropriate openings, with the scissors. Return your kit to the hanger and suspend in your chosen spot.

Follow the care instructions for the mushrooms in your grow-at-home kit. When your mushrooms are ready to harvest, be sure to gather all of them before removing the kit from the macramé hanger.

TIP As macramé is a simple but effective craft, you could design and make your own macramé hanger. Depending on the style of your hanger, consider top fruiting or side fruiting your mushrooms.

Vase of Mushrooms

How to grow your own bouquet of mushrooms

In this project we encourage you to enjoy the ornamental beauty of mushrooms as they grow in a vase of your choice, nestled among your houseplants. By exploiting the variety of colours available in mushrooms, you can add a whole new dimension to your indoor plant display.

WHEN This is a great all-season indoor project, so you can enjoy a stunning display of mushrooms year-round.

WHERE A location that is visually prominent and in a room you use often. Oyster mushrooms grow rapidly, so why not position them where you can watch the mushrooms evolve throughout their life cycle.

Method

Getting started

Thoroughly clean and dry your vase; then lightly disinfect its inside with alcohol spray and leave to dry. Spray the inside of the bowl that you will use to weigh and rehydrate your pellets also, and again leave to dry.

Remove your spawn from the fridge and leave to acclimatize. Weigh out your pellets and place in the bowl and add your water. The pellets will absorb up to one and a half times their weight in liquid, and will double in size. Leave the mixture to stand for about 20 minutes, until all the water has been absorbed. Then break up the pellets with a clean fork and mix in your spawn. Add the spawn-and-pellet mixture to your vase, and gently press it down. Be careful not to compact your mixture as this will prevent air circulating around the spawn and affect its healthy growth.

Once your container is filled to the top, place it in the cardboard box and close it over: this is to create a dark space. Store the box in a steady temperature of 17–20°C (63–68°F).

Check your vase every week to make sure the mycelium is growing – you will begin to see the white of the mycelium consuming your substrate during this period.

MUSHROOMS

Black pearl oyster (*Pleurotus ostreatus × P. eryngii*)

Grey oyster (*Pleurotus ostreatus*)

Pink oyster (*Pleurotus djamor*)

Yellow oyster (*Pleurotus citrinopileatus*)

MATERIALS

• 1 litre (1¾ pint) vase with narrow opening

• Alcohol spray

• Bowl large enough to take the pellets once rehydrated

• 100g (3½oz) mushroom spawn, keep refrigerated until needed and check storage instructions for spawn storage with your supplier.

• 250g (8oz) hardwood or straw pellets

• 365ml (13fl. oz) cold water

• Fork

• Cardboard box, big enough to fit your vase

Mister/spray bottle

Incubation period

After 21 days, your substrate will be fully colonized, that is completely covered in white, fluffy mycelium. Bring your vase out into the light and give the opening a good mist with fresh water. There may be some mycelium growing over and around the outside of the vase, you can simply wipe this away with clean hands, but make sure not to disturb the mycelium around the opening of your vase. Pour away any standing water that pools in the top of the vase.

Mist your vase at least twice a day, and more frequently on hot and sunny days. After 10–12 days, you should see your mushrooms beginning to form. Once fully grown, harvest the entire bouquet for eating.

Getting more from your vase

After you've harvested your first batch of mushrooms, you can leave your vase *in situ* and continue to mist twice a day. After a couple of weeks, you might begin to see a second flush of growth.

If the white mycelium remains visibly healthy, you will continue to get a few flushes of mushrooms from your vase. Each flush may take longer to appear and may produce fewer mushrooms each time, but you can go on displaying it until there are no more.

If your substrate begins to look dry or turns brown or green, this means the mycelium is likely to be at the end of its life and could be contaminated. It's unlikely you'll see another flush of mushrooms, and so this is a good time to restore your vase.

Restoring your vase

Soaking your vase in water is the best way to soften the substrate inside, making it easier to remove. The substrate can go on to your garden soil, on to your compost pile or simply be disposed of it as you would your normal food waste.

TIP Consider having a variety of vases with different oyster mushroom spawns, but don't mix your spawns: keep one type to one vase at a time.

Growing on Jeans
Upcycling with a twist

Oyster mushrooms are one of the world's great recyclers and they will thrive on many different mediums in the right conditions. In this project we show you how to get them growing on a pair of old jeans. However, this is just an example of material that you might use. Feel free to experiment with any number of fabrics – old jumpers or worn-out towels. Whatever you choose, make sure the material is made of natural fibres and pasteurized, as shown here.

WHEN Year-round.

WHERE You need to leave your kit to inoculate for 21 days in the dark, at a constant temperature of 17–20 °C (63–68 °F). Place your inoculated jeans in a bright spot in clear view, so that you remember to water it and can watch it grow. Next to the kitchen sink or on a shaded windowsill are good options.

Method

Getting started
Wash and dry your hands, work surfaces and equipment to reduce the risk of contamination.

Place your clean jeans in the heatproof basin and cover them with boiling water. You should completely submerge all the jean material. Use a wooden spoon or tongs to press your jeans below the surface of the water. Leave to cool.

Meanwhile, remove your bag of spawn from the fridge and allow it to reach room temperature. While keeping the bag sealed, give its contents a squeeze to break up the spawn.

Once the water and the jeans are cool enough to handle, empty the excess water from the bowl, and leave the jeans to drain for a few minutes. With clean hands, roll the jeans up and give them a good squeeze, so they don't drip when held up.

Lie the jeans flat on a clean surface. Spread half of the spawn along one-half of the jeans. Distribute the spawn evenly across

MUSHROOMS

Grey oyster (*Pleurotus ostreatus*)

Pink oyster (*Pleurotus djamor*)

Yellow oyster (*Pleurotus citrinopileatus*)

MATERIALS

- Pair of clean old jeans*
- Heatproof container, large enough to submerge your jeans into
- Boiling water
- Wooden spoon or tongs
- 200g (7oz) oyster mushroom grain spawn, kept refrigerated until needed
- 2 pairs of medium-sized rubber bands or 2 pieces of string 30cm (12in) long
- Mushroom growbag with filter patch
- Sticky tape, to seal your growbag
- Mister/spray bottle
- Scissors (optional)
- Plate (optional)

*Ensure no paint, dyes, recent chemical treatments have been used on the fabric because of the risk of bioaccumulation.

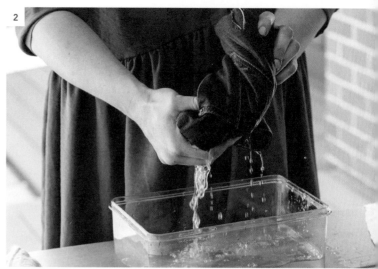

the leg all the way up to the waistband. Fold the jeans in half lengthways, then repeat using the remaining spawn across the second leg.

Once the spawn is evenly distributed, roll the jeans from the bottom of the trouser legs all the way up to the waistband. Loosely tie the strings around the jean roll or use the rubber bands to hold it together. Then place the jean roll in your growbag, which should fit loosely around the jeans – spawn is a living organism that needs a good supply of oxygen to thrive. Seal the growbag by folding the top over a couple of times and use the tape to hold it in place.

Place your growbag in a dark location. The ideal temperature for this phase of the project is 17–20°C (63–68°).

To initiate fruiting

After 21 days, the material should be fully colonized; your jeans will be covered in a layer of white mycelium. Place them – still in the growbag – into your fridge for about 24 hours. This will cold-shock your kit into fruiting.

After that you need to introduce light, oxygen and humidity to your jean roll to help initiate fruiting. Remove your jean roll from the fridge and take it out of the growbag; alternatively, you can cut the growbag away from the jeans with clean scissors.

Place your jean roll on a plate or other clean surface and put it in a light airy spot, where you will remember to spray it with water twice a day. Always spray more regularly in warmer weather. Once the little pins (primordia) begin to show, your mushrooms will grow rapidly. Continue spraying them twice a day, to avoid them drying out.

Harvesting your mushrooms

Your mushrooms should be ready to harvest 5–7 days after they first appear. Do this when their caps start flattening out. To remove, pinch and twist close to the base of each cluster.

There is not much nutrition in a pair of jeans, so you will get only one harvest of mushrooms from this project.

TIP After you've finished with your grow kit, consider burying your jeans in the garden – unroll and cover with a shallow layer of topsoil or mulch. This will allow the mycelium to gather more nutrients and potentially prompt the growth of more mushrooms in your garden. Alternatively, your jean roll can go straight into your compost bin.

Grow Your Own Seed Pots

Homemade, plastic-free seed pots

Out with the plastic and in with the mycelium, which is the vegetive body of the mushroom. In this project, it forms and binds with a substrate mix to create beautiful pots to support your freshly sown seeds as they develop. When your seedlings are ready to plant, the pots will compost down, turning into food for worms and nourishing your soil.

WHEN Any time of the year. The pots will take ten days to complete.

WHERE This is a kitchen-based project, but you will need to store your pots for up to a week in the dark.

MUSHROOMS

Grey oyster (*Pleurotus* spp.)

Reishi (*Ganoderma lingzhi*)

MATERIALS

(for six seed pots)

• Alcohol spray

• Muffin tin

• Large bowl

• 300g (10oz) hardwood fuel pellets

• 500ml (17½fl. oz) cold water

• 75g (3oz) flour

• 250g (9oz) mushroom spawn, kept refrigerated until needed

• Baking paper, clingfilm or beeswax paper, to cover your muffin tray

• Cardboard box, big enough to fit your muffin tray

• Baking tray

Method

Getting started

Ensure you have clean hands and work surfaces. Sterilize your muffin tin with your alcohol spray and leave to dry.

In a bowl, rehydrate your pellets with the cold water; this will take approximately thirty minutes. Once the pellets have absorbed all the water, mix in the flour and the spawn.

Then line the inside of your muffin tin wells with your baking paper, clingfilm or beeswax paper. Add your mixture to each well. Press the mixture into the base and sides of the wells, ensuring the walls of each are lined with an even layer, around 1cm (⅜in) thick. Make sure you build the sides nice and high, as the pots will reduce in size by approx. 10 per cent as they dry. Then place a layer of baking paper, clingfilm or beeswax paper over the top of your formed seed pots.

Put your muffin tin into the cardboard box, and close. Store in a dark place while the mycelium within your mixture grows, binding the ingredients together.

Incubation period

After five days, you should see a good amount of white fluffy mycelium covering your substrate mix. With clean hands, carefully lift off the top layer of baking paper, clingfilm or beeswax paper and remove the seed pots from your muffin tin. They should be firm to the touch but could be a bit fragile at this stage. Peal the baking paper, cling film or beeswax paper from the base of the pots.

Place your seed pots on a clean baking tray, and put them back inside the cardboard box and return to the dark spot for another three days. This will allow the mycelium to fully colonize the substrate.

Once this has occurred, remove your pots from the cardboard box and place them on a clean baking tray. Preheat your oven to 140°C (275°F; gas mark 1), and once at the correct temperature put the baking tray with the seed pots in the oven and bake for forty-five minutes.

Remove and leave to completely cool. Once cool, your seed pots are ready to fill.

TIP Adapt this process to make mushroom-based packaging that can replace not-so-Earth-friendly polystyrene. A simple mould can be made from any solid form, such as a loaf tin. The white mycelium that forms on your substrate is water-resistant, and the process of oven drying will stop any mushrooms from growing.

Spore Prints

Create stunning prints using mushroom spores

A spore print is a helpful way to identify a mushroom – it's like a mushroom's fingerprint. Here we show you how to capture your own unique and delicate spore prints using a variety of papers, mushrooms and coloured spores.

Mushroom spores are released from the gills on the underside of a mature gilled mushroom. There are thousands of mushroom spores floating around you at any one time. Being microscopic in size, they go mostly unnoticed – travelling on the breeze and on animals in the hope that they'll settle in the right spot.

The colour of a mushroom's gills will indicate what colour their spores are likely to be. The white or pale gills of grey oyster mushrooms will appear white; the mid-brown gills of a portobello mushroom will appear brown. Pink oyster mushrooms will give you a delicately pale pink spore print.

Select a contrasting colour for your paper base, to make striking and interesting prints – feel free to experiment, too.

WHEN This project can be done at any time of the year with fresh, home-grown, shop-brought or even foraged mushrooms that have reached maturity.

WHERE A calm, draught-free environment where you can leave your mushrooms to rest without being disturbed.

Method

Getting started

Make sure your mushrooms are at room temperature. Place one mushroom gill-side down on your paper or card. Repeat with other mushrooms, according to your design. Cover with a bowl and leave.

After 2–6 hours, carefully lift the bowl and delicately peel the mushrooms off the paper or card. Fix the spore print in place with a light spray of fixer.

MUSHROOMS

Lion's mane or any fresh gilled mushroom from the Mushroom Directory (see pages 160–185)

MATERIALS

- 4–6 fresh, gilled mature mushrooms
- Bowl to cover mushrooms
- Artist fixing spray or hairspray
- Small bowl of fresh water (optional)

THE PRINT BASE OPTIONS

- Black or white card
- Brown paper or card
- Glass such as microscope slides
- Heavy paper in a variety of colours
- Tin foil

TIP Overmature or under-mature mushrooms won't produce any spores and so won't leave a print. It's difficult to guess what stage shop-bought mushrooms are at. You can try dampening the cap with a wet finger, to encourage under-mature mushrooms to drop their spores.

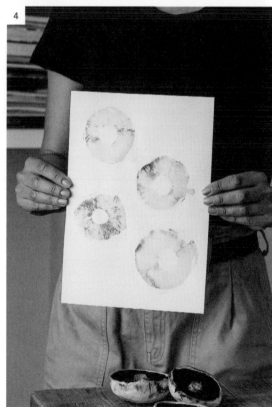

Log Project

Growing mushrooms on logs, an outdoor project

Growing mushrooms on logs is a classic technique that imitates the natural growing environment in which many of our edible, saprotrophic mushrooms thrive in the wood and forests around us.

The density of the hardwood and freshness of the logs means the mycelium has a wealth of nutrients in store and so will continue to fruit for many years, giving you a steady supply of fresh and home-grown mushrooms.

To give your mushrooms the best chance of survival, select a log from a healthy hardwood or fruit tree with its bark still intact. We recommend freshly harvested logs, no older than 6–8 weeks, to avoid potential contamination with another type of fungus.

You should inoculate your log with only one type of mushroom spawn (see page 29). You can get summer and winter variants for many of the log-growing mushrooms, so ask your dowel supplier which variant they can supply to determine what you'd like to grow.

WHEN Logs can be inoculated throughout the year.

WHERE Place your log somewhere outdoors, sheltered from harsh winds and direct sunshine, but exposed to rain. During dry weeks and in warmer weather, water your logs as you would your plants. If your log dries out, the mycelium is likely to perish and your log will not fruit.

MUSHROOMS

Lion's mane *(Hericium erinaceus)*

Grey oyster *(Pleurotus ostreatus)*

Shiitake *(Lentinula edodes)*

Velvet shank *(Flammulina velutipes)*

MATERIALS

• Hardwood log, min. 50cm (20in) long and 12–20cm (5–8in) diameter
• 30 pre-inoculated dowels
• Drill bit of the same diameter as your inoculated dowels
• Alcohol sanitizer wipes or spray
• Pen or tape
• Drill with a hammer function
• Hammer
• Heat source to melt your wax
• 50g (2oz) soy wax - or beeswax
• Soft sponge dabber or a paintbrush, to apply the melted wax
• Self-adhesive label
• Knife or scissors (optional)

Method

Getting started

Take your log and set it on a table or workbench. Remove your inoculated dowels from the fridge. Clean your drill bit with sanitizer or boiling water.

Mark your drill bit with a pen or a length of tape to the same depth as your dowels. This is to ensure you get evenly drilled holes, no deeper than your dowels.

With the pen, mark your first row with five points evenly spaced in a straight line along the length of your log. For the next row, offset your holes from the first row – this will eventually give you a diamond figuration around your log and ensure even colonization of the mycelium. For your thirty dowels, you need to mark six rows of five points.

Drill your holes where marked, to the depth of your pen mark or tape. Place a dowel into a hole and hammer it in until it is flush with the surface of the log. Do this for all thirty dowels.

Warm the wax until it has all melted, then leave it over a low heat. Using the sponge dabber or paintbrush, cover the tops of the dowels and any wounds from cut branches with the melted wax to seal them. Sealing helps to protect your dowels from squirrels and insects during the incubation period. Do not seal the two cut ends of your log; these should be left open to allow for water absorption. Mark your log so that it can be readily identified. You need to be able to identify the mushrooms growing from your log, too. Then place your log in a shaded spot, lying it down, standing it on its end or leaning it against a support.

Keep checking on your log for signs of fruiting and to make sure it isn't drying out. If there is no rainfall for a week, or if your log is sheltered from the rain, remember to water it weekly with a watering can or hose.

You can expect to see your first mushrooms after 9–12 months. However, mushroom varieties differ in how long they take to fully inoculate a log. It also depends on the size of your log.

Harvesting your mushrooms

We recommend harvesting your mushrooms when they are still young, to ensure they are fresh and delicious. To do this, pinch the mushrooms at their base close to the log and twist. Alternatively, you can cut your mushrooms off with a knife or scissors.

TIP
When growing outdoors there is a risk of wild spores colonizing your substrate so be sure to check the caps, gills and stems for similarities or variants.

Straw Bales

Growing on straw bales prepared with chicken wire and spawn

One of the quickest and simplest ways to cultivate mushrooms is to grow them on straw, and it's also super low-maintenance. Constructing and filling your straw bale should take roughly one hour (less if you've got someone helping you), and with regular watering you should see your first mushrooms sprout within 6–8 weeks.

WHEN We'd suggest setting up in spring, once there is minimal risk of frost, or during autumn, at least six weeks before the frosts return. This gives your bale good time to establish ahead of the cold season. If you're wanting to grow pink oyster mushrooms, we'd recommend starting them in late spring as they like warmer weather.

WHERE A shaded area away from direct sunlight – under a tree or behind a shed –is perfect, but a flower bed or shady spot in your allotment would work, too. Make sure it's easily accessible so you can water the straw bale during drier weather.

Method

Getting started
Take your fresh sawdust spawn out of the fridge and leave to acclimatize for an hour or so. While this is occurring, you can prepare the chosen area for your straw bale. Clear the ground of any debris and make sure you'll be able to access the bale from all sides.

To begin, using the tape measure and your scissors cut two circular bases, 80cm (32in) in diameter, from your cardboard sheets; these should match the diameter of your chicken wire collar (see below). Place one circular base on top of the other for a double layer. Put the base in position, choose a shaded area away from direct sunlight and give it a good water, making sure both layers are soaked through.

Then construct your chicken wire collar using the protective gloves and wires cutter. These instructions allow for a chicken wire collar 80cm (32in) high and approx. 80cm (32in) in diameter, but you

MUSHROOMS

Grey oyster (*Pleurotus ostreatus*)
Italian oyster (*Pleurotus pulmonarius*)
Pearl oyster (*Pleurotus ostreatus*)
Pink oyster (*Pleurotus djamor*)*

* Recommended only for late spring–summer inoculation

MATERIALS

- 3kg (6½lb) fresh, oyster mushroom sawdust spawn, refrigerated
- Tape measure
- Scissors
- Ink- and tape-free cardboard to cover the base with 1–2 layers
- Watering can or hose
- Chicken wire or similar, approx. 80 × 150cm (32 × 60in)
- Wire cutters
- Protective gloves
- 15kg (33lb) untreated straw (not hay)
- Rake or broom (optional)

can tailor these measurements to the area you have available. If the collar becomes too tall and wide, you run the risk of it being unstable when in situ and soaked with water. Wrap your chicken wire to form a cylinder of 80cm (32in) diameter. Fix in place by twisting in the loose ends of the wire to the cylinder. Then continue to wrap the remaining length of wire around the first layer of wire, forming a two-layer collar. Secure by twisting the loose wire ends round the body of the cylinder.

Put your chicken wire collar on top of the cardboard and check that the size and location feel right before you start to fill it with straw. Start with a 20cm- (8in-) deep layer of straw, compacting it down as best you can – using a broom or rake is really helpful here. Use clean hands to scatter and spread about 500g (1lb) sawdust spawn evenly over the top of the straw, breaking up any lumps and making sure it reaches the edges of the bale. Then add another layer of straw and of spawn. Repeat until you have six layers of straw, with your sawdust spawn divided between them. Finish with a generous layer of straw. Then gently push the top layer of straw down and spray the whole bale with water until the bale is damp but not soaked. Do not overwater at this stage, as this could cause the sawdust spawn to wash out of the sides and base.

Over the next 3–4 weeks the spawn will inoculate the straw layers. Keep spraying your bale during drier periods and warmer weather, ensuring it doesn't dry out. If there's a chance of frost, hold off on the watering; otherwise you could cause the bale to freeze.

Harvesting your mushrooms

After 6–8 weeks you should start to see your mushrooms beginning to fruit. Be sure to check all around your bale, as they have a tendency to pop up where you least expect. Your bale will continue to fruit for the next few months if conditions allow. Pink and Italian oyster mushrooms prefer warmer weather, whereas other species will fruit during the milder seasons.

Pick your mushrooms early to avoid bugs getting there first, and keep checking regularly for growth. When you spot a mushroom that is ready to harvest, hold the cluster firmly in your hand, pinch close to the base and gently twist. It will tear away from the straw easily.

TIP Over the course of twelve months the straw will begin to compact down and decompose, but you can keep topping it up with more layers of clean straw and fresh sawdust spawn every few months.

Shed Growing
Growing your own button mushrooms

Growing and harvesting your own button mushrooms is another delightfully simple project. They don't need light to grow, so this method allows you to utilize unused space in your shed.

Button mushrooms enjoy nitrogen-rich compost. You can source ready-made, manure-based or peat-free compost from your local garden centre. With this project you can have mushrooms growing within a couple of months, and deliciously fresh mushrooms popping up for weeks more.

Button mushrooms have a subtle sweet flavour and firm texture, and are super tasty when thinly sliced and eaten raw. You will marvel at how delicious this simple dinner staple can be when home harvested.

WHEN Wait until spring to begin as the mushrooms enjoy warmer weather. If you want to continue growing through summer, make sure your shed is shaded and temperatures don't exceed 23°C (73°F).

WHERE A dark corner in a shed is perfect. If growing indoors, a dark cupboard, basement or under the stairs will also work. You need a steady temperature of 15–20°C (59–68°F). If it is any cooler, mycelium growth will be slow and you risk contamination; if above 23°C (73°F), you risk killing the spawn.

MUSHROOMS

Button (*Agaricus bisporus* var. *bisporus*)

Common brown (*Agaricus bisporus* var. *hortensis*)

Cremini (*Agaricus bisporus* var. *bisporus*)

Portobello (*Agaricus bisporus*)

White/Closed cap (*Agaricus bisporus* var. *bisporus*)

MATERIALS

• Container 35–40 × 25–30 × min. 15cm (14–16 × 10–12 × 6in)

• Approx. 4kg (9lb) manure or peat-free compost

• 1kg (2¼lb) mushroom spawn – *Agaricus bisporus* var. *bisporus* (for white mushrooms) or *Agaricus bisporus* var. *hortensis* (for common brown mushrooms)

• Newspaper

• Mister/spray bottle

FOR THE CASING LAYER

• 250g (9oz) rehydrated coco coir

• 250g (9oz) vermiculite

Method

Getting started

Make sure your box is clean and dry. Then fill your container with compost up to one-third from the top, and add your spawn. Make sure it's well mixed in with your compost, and the spawn is evenly distributed.

Wet your newspaper under the tap and lay over the top of your substrate. Leave the container in a shed to incubate for three weeks, in a temperature of 15–18°C (59–65°F). Keep the newspaper damp by spraying it as and when it dries out.

Over the three weeks of incubation, if you have a peek under the newspaper, you should expect to see the fine white hyphae spreading across your compost. This is the mycelium colonizing your substrate. Once it is fully colonized and you can see a good amount of white mycelium growth in the compost, it is time to add a casing layer to the top of your substrate. This process will encourage your mushrooms to fruit.

Fruiting your mushrooms

When ready, remove the newspaper layer and discard. Hydrate your coco coir as per the instructions on the packaging. Mix the hydrated coco coir and vermiculite together and spread a layer, 3cm (1¼in) deep, over the top of your substrate.

Spray the top of the mixture so it's damp but not dripping if squeezed. We call this level of hydration 'field capacity'. If the substrate is too wet, your mycelium will drown; if too dry, it could perish.

Move your container, uncovered, to a dark spot and make sure to maintain the field-capacity level of hydration in the top casing layer throughout the fruiting period through frequent spraying with a mister.

Harvesting your mushrooms

Once you see your mushrooms beginning to grow, they'll take a few days to reach 'baby mushroom' size, which is 1–2cm (½–¾in) wide. Harvest them one at a time, picking each one from the base, and making sure to cover the harvested spot with the surrounding casing layer, using your fingers.

Your mushrooms will continue to pop up sporadically for a number of weeks, so continue to keep the casing layer moist during this period.

TIP Once your mushrooms have finished growing, recycle the spent substrate, which is a great soil conditioner and well worth also adding to your garden pots or vegetable beds. For more ideas, see Mycovermicomposting (page 128).

Greenhouse or Polytunnel Growing

Cultivating mushrooms in your greenhouse

The warmth and shelter of a greenhouse or polytunnel is a great environment in which to grow mushrooms when the weather has turned cold. These mushroom growbags will happily sit under a workbench, growing slowly and giving you fresh fruiting mushrooms for a good few months.

WHEN This is a good project to get going in early spring or in late autumn.

WHERE The extra space under a greenhouse workbench, or on some shelves while they are free of seedlings.

MUSHROOMS

Grey oyster (*Pleurotus ostreatus*)
Italian oyster (*Pleurotus pulmonarius*)
Pearl oyster (*Pleurotus ostreatus*)
White oyster (*Pleurotus cornucopiae*)

MATERIALS

- 3kg (6½lb) straw
- 2 netted bags/onion bags, approx. 30 × 45cm (12 × 18in)
- 2 large buckets
- Strong protective gloves
- Face mask
- 50g (2oz) hydrated lime (with low magnesium)
- 0.75–1kg (1½–2¼lb) fresh sawdust spawn, kept refrigerated until needed
- Brown-paper, 25kg (55lb) potato sack, approx. 85 × 30cm (34 × 12in)
- Strong tape or string, 1m (3ft) long
- Sharp knife or scissors
- Mister/spray bottle

Method

Getting started

To pasteurize your straw, divide it into the two netted bags. Fill each bucket with clean water to about 60 per cent full. Don gloves and a facemask before handling your lime, and mixing it with the water. You will need to add ½ tsp of lime for every litre (1¾ pints) of water you use.

Submerge the bags containing the straw in the lime water mix, weighing down each bag and making sure they're fully covered. Leave to soak.

After 12 hours, remove the straw-filled netted bags from the lime water and hang up and leave to drip-drain for an hour. Discard the lime water and rinse your bucket clean.

Empty all of your straw back into a clean dry bucket. Add your spawn and, with clean hands, mix the straw and spawn thoroughly. Once fully combined, empty your straw and spawn mix into your potato sack. Try not to compact the straw. When filled, loosely fold the top section of the potato sack down twice. There's no need to seal it– airflow is essential to support mycelium growth – but you need to ensure the potato sack isn't gaping open either, as this may lead to the substrate drying out. Store the substrate-filled potato sack in a greenhouse or polytunnel.

Initiating growth

After 3–4 weeks, you will hopefully see a healthy growth of white mycelium binding your straw substrate together. You may even notice signs of the mycelium on the outside of the potato sack. You now want to remove the air from the top of the sack. To do this, fold the top of the sack down as far as the substrate will let you and tape or tie it closed.

With a sharp knife or scissors, carefully cut a 15cm (6in) 'X' shape in one side of the potato sacks, and make three further incisions at even intervals around the sack. Spray the openings with clean water and place your sack in a greenhouse or polytunnel. Repeat once a day; during warmer weather, you should spray them more often. Over the next 2–4 weeks you should start to see your mushrooms popping through the openings. Keep spraying them until they're fully grown, and the caps begin to flatten out.

Harvesting your mushrooms

Pinch each mushroom at the base and lift it away from the substrate. Make sure you harvest all the mushrooms within each opening at once. This will allow the substrate to recover, and you could get a second or third crop within the next couple of months. Keep spraying the openings and checking all around the sack for new signs of growth.

TIP Once your bag has stopped fruiting, you can put it and the substrate mix straight into your compost, which will help to nourish and condition your soil. Alternatively, spread the contents over your vegetable patch, around your strawberries or flower beds – this will give the mycelium a chance to recharge, and you may see more mushrooms popping up in your garden.

Mushroom Beds

Growing kings in your garden

Why not utilize those shady areas in your garden while improving your soil's diversity and adding variety to your garden growing? This easy project, which requires very little maintenance, is perfect for cultivating the king stropharia mushroom – a fantastic beginners' mushroom – in your mushroom bed.

WHEN Lay your mushroom bed once there is minimal risk of frost in late spring and before frosts restart in autumn. This will allow your mycelium network plenty of time to establish. King stropharia mushrooms tend to fruit in autumn, when evenings are cooler and rain is more frequent, although that's not to say that they won't pop up in earlier in the year if the weather suits.

WHERE Find a shaded spot in your garden with room for a 2 × 1m (7 × 3ft) rectangular bed. The bed must contain well-drained soil – avoid any areas that collect standing water during periods of sustained rainfall. That said, the mushroom bed should also be within reach of a water supply so that the soil doesn't dry out during summer.

MUSHROOMS

King stropharia (*Stropharia rugosoannulata*)

MATERIALS

• Ink- and tape-free cardboard, to cover 8sq. m (86sq. ft) of earth
• Watering can fitted with a rose or a hose with a spray attachment
• 3kg (6½lb) king stropharia sawdust spawn, kept refrigerated until needed
• 12kg (26lb) untreated chopped straw
• 200 litres (352 pints) fresh untreated woodchip (no more than three months old)

Method

Getting started

Mark out the size of your bed, and level any dirt so the ground is even. Lay down your cardboard in two layers and then water until the cardboard is completely saturated.

Spread half of your straw in an even layer on top of the cardboard and then distribute half of your spawn over the straw. Cover with the remaining straw, and crumble the rest of your spawn over that. Top with an even layer of woodchip. By adding this layer, you could get a bountiful harvest of these delicious garden giants in just a few months; the layer of woodchip is needed to nourish the mycelium for this particular strain of mushroom and it also helps prevent the bed from drying out.

Water your bed until it is throughly soaked. Take care not to overwater as this will wash your spawn away.

Initiating growth

Check your bed every week to monitor moisture levels, as well as mycelium growth. When watering, take care not to saturate the soil as this will create an anaerobic environment, which is ideal for bacteria that could damage your mycelium. The bark layer you have added will help it retain a good level of moisture below, as well as feeding your mycelium.

Replenish the top layer of woodchip each spring or to ensure your mycelium has plenty of nutrition. If fruiting has been slow or tailed off, during the following spring spread 500g (1lb) fresh sawdust spawn, and apply a new layer of woodchip.

Harvesting your mushrooms

Cut these mushrooms, with their distinctive reddish caps, at the base with a knife, or use your hands to twist them loose. Harvest while young and before the caps open too wide; after this, the mushrooms can disintegrate quickly.

TIP It's likely to take about 6–9 months before you see lots of healthy mycelial growth throughout the bed – pretty soon after that you will see mushrooms coming through.

Companion Planting

Growing mushrooms among your existing plants and vegetables

Companion planting is about creating dynamic and mutually beneficial planting combinations to help your garden thrive. In this instance, we're going to show you how you can grow mushrooms among your edible and ornamental plants. They will help to nourish your plants, trees, vegetables and soil – and you, too.

Mushrooms have a fascinating relationship with plants and trees – it's called a symbiotic relationship, meaning it's mutually beneficial. By introducing a healthy network of mycelium into your garden you can increase the biodiversity of your soil. Mycelium helps to break down organic matter, releasing nutrients back into the soil. It also helps your soil maintain its moisture levels, and prevents erosion from heavy rainfall. Mycelium attracts bountiful worms; their movement through the soil helps aerate it, while their casts (excrement) act as a fertilizer. A diverse and varied soil will see an increased harvest in fruit and vegetables and larger flower yields, plus your garden will be better protected against drought and flooding.

WHEN We suggest laying your mushroom substrate down in spring, once there is minimal risk of frost and before your bedding plants or vegetables start filling out

WHERE The idea behind companion planting is to distribute your substrate layers in and around garden foliage and/or vegetable plants. The area should be protected from direct sunlight, as well as being accessible for watering and harvesting.

MUSHROOMS

Grey oyster (*Pleurotus ostreatus*)
Italian oyster (*Pleurotus pulmonarius*)
King stropharia (*Stropharia rugosoannulata*)
Pearl oyster (*Pleurotus ostreatus*)
White oyster (*Pleurotus cornucopiae*)

MATERIALS

- 3kg (6½lb) fresh sawdust spawn of your chosen mushroom, kept refrigerated until needed
- 9kg (20lb) untreated straw (not hay) – enough to cover an area of 3sq. m (32sq. ft)
- Woodchip or other type of organic mulch, to cover 3sq. m (32sq. ft) to a depth of 3cm (1¼in)
- Hose with a fine sprinkler attachment

Method

Getting started

Take your fresh sawdust spawn out of the fridge and leave to acclimatize for an hour or so while you prepare the area (here, 1m x 2m/3¼ft x 6½ft) for your substrate layers by clearing the ground of any debris. Then cover the area with your straw. With clean hands, scatter half of your spawn evenly over the top of the straw, breaking up any lumps and making sure it reaches the edges of your area. Add another layer of straw and sprinkle the rest of your spawn on top of that, and then finish with a generous layer of straw.

Once you have even layers of straw and sawdust spawn, you can cover the whole area with your woodchips or other type of organic mulch. Make sure it's an even layer, and that it covers all the straw.

Lightly water the area with the fine sprinkler setting on your hose. You need only to dampen the woodchip as the water will work its way down through the straw. Do not flood the area as this may wash away the sawdust spawn.

Maintenance

Over the following 3–4 weeks, the spawn will colonize the straw layers. Keep spraying your substrate during drier spells, to ensure it doesn't dry out. Also note that, if there is a chance of frost, it is best to avoid watering as this will cause the substrate to freeze.

Harvesting your mushrooms

After a further 8–12 weeks (temperate weather permitting), you will start to see your oyster mushrooms beginning to fruit – be sure to check for them everywhere, especially under shadier areas. Harvest them as their caps begin to flatten out, picking the whole cluster at once. If you want to harvest when your mushrooms are young, and before the bugs get to them, they'll still be delicious. Simply pinch at the base and lift away from the straw and mulch.

King stropharia mushrooms will take longer to establish, and you should see them begin to fruit in autumn when planted in spring. Harvest them also when the caps begin to flatten out.

Your mushrooms will continue to fruit, when the conditions allow, for the next few months, and until the temperatures drop.

TIP Over the following 12–18 months the straw will begin to compact down and decompose. You can add a fresh layer of spawn and mulch the following spring.

Crops in Pots

No-garden gardening for mushrooms

Here's a chance to get more out of your used mushroom kit and to nourish your potted plants, balcony containers or patio planters at the same time. Instead of composting or otherwise disposing of spent mushroom substrate with your usual food waste, in this project you can repurpose it, kicking the mycelium back into action and spurring it on to fruit again. Although the nutrients within a used mushroom kit have been depleted, it's still teaming with living mycelium so it would be a shame to let this go to waste.

If you have access to spent substrate sourced directly from a mushroom farm, you can repurpose larger amounts by breaking it up and spreading it directly on top of your plant pots or containers. The thicker the substrate layer, the better chance it has of surviving and not drying out. Make sure to keep it watered and damp, especially during drier spells.

By following the growing guidelines for your plants, the mushrooms will successfully grow alongside them quite happily. If you find mushrooms growing, be sure to identify them correctly before harvesting – checking their caps, gills, stems and spores. Make sure they match the mushrooms you intended to grow.

WHEN This project can be done at any time of the year. If you choose summer, make sure you are able to water your pots often to prevent them from drying out.

WHERE No garden, no problem. You can put your used substrate into any pot or container filled with potting compost. And containers can be situated conveniently close to the house, so you'll be sure not to miss any mushrooms when they do pop up.

MUSHROOMS

Oyster (*Pleurotus* spp.)

MATERIALS

- Spent mushroom substrate
- Pots or other containers
- Potting compost or soil
- Mister/spray bottle (optional)

Method

Before you begin

You can use any substrate in this project, but the grey oyster variety is the most resilient and more likely to grow more mushrooms, other varieties might not be fruitful.

Getting started

Remove all the packaging from your mushroom grow kit. Fill some pots with potting compost or soil, or use existing potted plants.

Divide the spent substrate block into large chunks, then bury it in the soil in each pot. Cover with more potting compost, 3cm (1 in) deep. Then water the substrate to rehydrate it. Do be mindful of overwatering your pots, though; you can use a mister to keep the substrate damp.

Harvesting your mushrooms

You should see mushrooms popping up within a few weeks of laying your substrate. To harvest, pinch each mushroom at its base and lift away from the soil.

TIP Introducing some red worms (*Eisenia fetida*) into your outside plant pots and containers will aid mycelium growth as well as aerate and nourish your soil. By increasing the biodiversity within your containers, you will have a healthier soil and happier plants.

Winter Mushroom Bed

Supercharging your veg beds over winter

In this project we show you how to utilize spent oyster mushroom substrate, a by-product of the mushroom-growing process that is teaming with living mycelium. Oyster mushrooms are some of nature's greatest decomposers, turning the natural litter of your vegetable beds into nutrients ready for next year's growing season. Adding a thick layer of spent mushroom substrate to your beds will aid the rebuilding of your soil structure and increase its biodiversity.

As it settles into your vegetable beds, the substrate will go on to gather more nutrients from your soil and in turn produce a wonderful harvest of winter mushrooms. You may also find over the following year that you have a greater yield from your vegetable beds, and see fewer weeds among your crops. It's a win-win.

WHEN Early winter, you can also add the substrate around existing plants while your winter vegetables are still growing.

WHERE Beds in which you grow vegetables.

MUSHROOMS

Grey oyster (*Pleurotus ostreatus*)

MATERIALS

• 10kg (22lb) oyster mushroom substrate, to cover 1sq m. (11sq. ft)
• Rake
• Watering can or hose

Method

Getting started

Apply a layer of substrate, 10cm (4in) thick, over the top of your soil, at a rate of 10kg (22lb) oyster mushroom substrate for every 1sq m. (11sq. ft) of bed. Press down with your hands or a rake.

Maintenance

Water your substrate regularly to keep it hydrated, but avoid watering if there's a chance of frost.

Harvesting your mushrooms

If the weather remains mild and humid, you could see oyster mushrooms beginning to fruit only a couple of weeks after adding your spent substrate to your beds. As the weather cools, your mushrooms will grow more slowly, producing beautiful dark caps that can grow quite large. They have a firmer texture when cooked, too.

Harvest your oyster mushrooms before their caps begin to flatten out, picking the whole cluster at once. Always make sure any mushrooms you gather from outdoors have been correctly identified. Make sure they are thoroughly cooked before eating.

TIP When ready to prepare your beds for your growing season, you can apply a new top layer of soil, or you can mix your mushroom substrate into your existing soil. Try not to over-till your soil – you want to preserve the mycelium network you have been growing during the winter.

Mushroom Totems
Creative growing for bigger mushrooms

The great thing about log totems is that they allow you to grow impressive mushrooms.

Totem growing consists of vertically stacking large discs of freshly felled logs one on top of the other. The totems have impressive stature and can add good height to the back of a flower bed or shady corner of your allotment. What's more, the larger logs take longer to decompose and so will keep nourishing your mycelium, popping out mushrooms for many years to come.

WHEN We suggest starting this project between late spring and mid-autumn; this will allow the mycelium to establish itself before the weather cools and slows growth for winter.

WHERE Your totem needs to be sheltered from extreme weather, such as drying winds or direct sunlight. Make sure you can provide it with water throughout the year, especially during dry periods. Your mushrooms are likely to pop up when you're not looking, so find a spot that is visible and accessible for picking. It should also be somewhere safe, so your stacked logs can't be climbed on or knocked over.

MUSHROOMS

Chicken of the woods (*Laetiporus sulphureus*)
Lion's mane (*Hericium erinaceus*)
Italian oyster (*Pleurotus pulmonarius*)
Maitake (*Grifola frondosa*)

MATERIALS

• 3 large discs of hardwood, approx. 25–30cm (10–12in) diameter and 20–25cm (8–10in) deep
• 3kg (6½lb) sawdust spawn
• 2 layers of cardboard cut to the diameter of your log discs
• Watering can or hose
• 2 old newspapers or a large paper sack
• 5m (16ft) string
• Scissors

Method

Getting started

Hardwood logs provide the best growing conditions for fungi to thrive. Oak (*Quercus*), poplar (*Populus*) or beech are good options. Ideally, source your three large hardwood discs from a wood merchant or tree surgeon as they will be able to cut them to the right size and from the same tree trunk. This will mean they stack evenly, giving you a stable totem. When choosing the size of your hardwood discs, remember you want them wide enough not to topple over, but not so too big that you can't lift them when stacking your totem.

On the day of construction

Take your fresh sawdust spawn out of the fridge and leave to acclimatize for an hour. Clear and level the area where you plan to place your totem. Ensure the bottom disc can be placed flat on the ground, making a good and sturdy base.

Place your cardboard rounds, cut to the same size as the discs, on the ground, and water them until soaked through. With clean hands, place 1kg (2¼lb) spawn on top of your cardboard base. Use your hands to shape and press the spawn down into the shape of the base, making sure the top is flat, level and even. Then place your first log disc in position on top of this spawn layer. Test its stability and make sure it is level. This is your totem base, and its stability depends on this key layer.

Using clean hands, place a further 1kg (2¼lb) spawn on top of your timber disc. Then, with your hands, shape and press the spawn down into the shape of the disc, making sure the top is flat, level and even. Repeat this process with your final 1kg (2¼lb) spawn and top timber disc.

You then need to add a protective layer to help prevent your sawdust spawn from washing away or drying out. Wrap your paper sack or the newspapers around the layers of spawn so it covers the spawn layer entirely. Using the scissors, cut the string and secure the paper in place, making sure it is tight around the log discs and not slicing into the spawn layer. Ensure all three layers of spawn are protected. Then water your entire totem. Soak the paper and log discs with the sprinkler setting on your hose or through the watering can rose.

Maintenance

Over the next year, water regularly during hotter periods so your totem doesn't dry out. You can check on the spawn and mycelium by peeking under the paper and making sure both are damp to the touch.

After about a year, when you unwrap the paper you should see a strong and firm white layer of mycelium where the sawdust and spawn layers are. If the weather is still hot at this point, keep the paper in place until the weather cools and the autumn rains come.

Harvesting your mushrooms

Your mushrooms will fruit when the weather changes, especially with the cooler nights and heavy rain of autumn. Keep an eye on your totem after periods of rainfall and a drop in temperature.

Gather your mushrooms when they are looking full in shape and still healthy. Insects like to feast on mushrooms, too, so check your crop for any critters trying their luck.

> **TIP** It's always best to correctly identify any mushrooms you harvest from the outdoors, checking their caps, stems, spores and smell as confirmation that they are edible. There are many 'false' species (see directory, pages 160–85). All mushrooms growing in such places must be cooked thoroughly.

Morel Beds
Growing with firepit ash

Expensive and exotic morel mushrooms have long been considered a fine food – for good reason. They are a delicious and prized gourmet mushroom with a deep nutty taste and firm texture. It can take anywhere between three and five years to establish your morel bed and get a good crop growing, so it's a long-term project and a challenge, but certainly not impossible and one that's definitely rewarding.

These instructions are based on the method perfected by Adrian Ogden of Gourmet Woodland Mushrooms, kindly shared here with his permission.

WHEN Plan and prepare to set up your morel bed after the last frost of late spring. This gives the mycelium the best chance of establishing itself before the heat of summer and the colder winter months. Morel mushrooms grow early in the year with their season beginning in April, so keep a watchful eye out for any popping up at that time.

WHERE These mushrooms need dappled shade in a cool spot. It's also important that your bed has sandy, well-draining soil. Ensure you have access to plenty of collected rainwater to keep your bed well hydrated during dry spells.

MUSHROOMS

Black morel (*Morchella angusticeps*)

MATERIALS

(for a bed 1 × 1m/3 × 3ft)

- 1–2 buckets of firepit ash from burnt hardwood wood – no treated timber, paper or cardboard or petrol-based fire lighters should be used in making the ash

- 1 bucket of fine sand should your soil require it (if you already have soil with sand content, you can skip this step)

- Bucket of garden compost

- 2kg (4½lb) morel-mushroom sawdust spawn, kept refrigerated until needed; avoid grain spawn, which can attract pests

- 2.5kg (5½lb) powdered gypsum

- Rake

- Rain water or watering can with a fine rose

- Approx. 0.1cu. m (3½cu. ft) elm or ash woodchips, to lay over the top of your morel bed

Method

Getting started

Your firepit ash should be made by burning different-sized lengths of untreated hardwood to replicate a forest fire. Set your fire in a safe environment and make sure you can tend it properly for the duration of the burn. Allow your firepit to cool for at least twenty-four hours once it's finished burning.

Clear the area for your morel bed of any debris, and level the soil. If needed, apply a layer of sand to the soil at this stage.

Making your morel bed

Evenly mix your garden compost, spawn, gypsum and buckets of ash on your bed area. Level out the mix with a rake or your hands. Water the bed with a fine mister or through the rose of a watering can. Cover the ash and spawn mix with your woodchips.

Maintenance

Lightly water the morel bed with rain water regularly, making sure it doesn't dry out. Always use a rose on your watering can so as not to wash the sawdust spawn out of the ash bed.

Each year after the morel fruiting season you will need to feed your morel bed, replenishing it with a fresh layer of woodchip and ash.

Harvesting your mushrooms

Morel mushrooms are notoriously early fruiters, and you should see your first mushrooms in late March or April. They should appear after sustained and heavy rainfall. To harvest them, pinch each stem at ground level until it comes away from the woodchips.

TIP Be mindful of false morels and seek guidance for true morel identification rules. Morels should be well cooked before consuming them.

Mycovermicomposting

Mushrooms and worms: a composting match made in heaven

Mycovermicomposting is a fantastic way to utilize your spent mushroom substrate and kitchen waste. 'Myco' indicates a fungus in Greek, and 'vermi' is from the Latin vermis ('worm'). This variation of cold composting focuses specifically on the benefits that worms and mushrooms bring to your soil.

While feasting on your kitchen scraps and fungal mycelium, worms will digest the residual nutrients and excrete 'castings' throughout your compost. These excreted castings are teaming with microbes and bacteria that accelerate the decomposing process, turning your scraps into a valuable product for your garden. We recommend sourcing tiger worms (*Eisenia fetida*) for this project. These small worms burrow vertically, pulling down surface detritus and helping distribute nutrients throughout the soil. There are many reputable and dedicated suppliers of specific composting worms readily available here in the UK.

WHEN You can start your mycovermicompost at any time of the year, but be mindful that in winter your worms will slow down and not process as much. In the warmer drier months, you will need to make sure your compost doesn't overheat or dry out.

WHERE You can use any compost bin or buy a specialist wormery. The location should be shaded and easily accessible, so that you can keep adding to it and check in on your worms from time to time.

MUSHROOMS

A variety of mushroom mycelium will bring biodiversity and richness to your soil, so any one or more spent substrates listed within our projects can be used for this composting project.

MATERIALS

- 1kg (2¼lb), min., spent mushroom substrate
- Standard compost bin or wormery (with lid)
- 250g (9oz), min., composting worms such as tiger or red worms (*Eisenia fetida*)
- Large, double-handful of plant-based kitchen scraps
- Large handful of garden soil
- Sawdust or brown cardboard/paper (optional)

Method

Getting started

Crumble your spent mushroom substrate into your compost bin or wormery. Then mix your food scraps and garden soil into the substrate – avoid adding dairy products, fatty foods or fish/meat as these will attract pests. The same with garden waste; it may take longer for the worms to work through the heavier materials. Add your worms and replace the lid.

Maintenance

As the worms begin to colonize the compost, their burrowing will create paths through the mix, aerating the compost and improving moisture retention. Keep topping up your compost with your plant-based kitchen scraps. If it begins to get too wet, give the substrate a good mix. Also, make sure your wormery is draining properly; you could add some sawdust or brown cardboard/paper to help with this.

Once your substrate has been completely broken down into a lovely, rich, brown and earthy-smelling compost, it can be added to your garden soil as a conditioner. Being abundant in minerals, it will feed your plants and vegetables, and the worms will continue to nourish and condition your soil. Hopefully you will see bigger yields in your produce, and a mass of flowers on your plants.

TIP Always leave 25 per cent of the content inside your compost bin or wormery when emptying. To begin again, add your kitchen scraps and any mushroom substrate as before, then continue the cycle.

Christmas Tree Project

Upcycling your Christmas tree in the New Year

We hate to see anything go to waste, and there's something particularly sad about all those Christmas trees that line the kerbs in the first week of the New Year. With this project you can give your real Christmas tree a little extra love and repurpose its trunk to grow delicious mushrooms.

Spruce, fir and other conifer trees have natural anti-fungal properties, meaning mushrooms find it difficult to colonize their logs, but there are three types of edible mushroom that have found a way: Italian oyster, nameko and shiitake.

WHEN The New Year is the perfect time to inoculate your tree, what with the abundance of unwanted Christmas trees around. Ideally, your used Christmas tree should have been cut down no more than eight weeks before starting this project and have no obvious signs of other fungal growth.

WHERE For storing your log after inoculation, find a sheltered spot in the garden or on a balcony with access to natural rainfall. Your log will need to be protected from extreme weather, as well as harsh winds.

Method

Getting started

When selecting the part of your Christmas tree to use, consider that your log should be a minimum of 8cm (3¼in) thick and 50cm (20in) long. For that size, we recommend 20–30 dowels. Thicker logs will require a higher concentration of dowels and could take longer to inoculate. As a rule of thumb: the more dowels, the quicker and stronger the inoculation.

To begin, cut the branches off the lower part of your tree. Remove them carefully and as close to the main trunk as possible. Then cut the trunk further up, to the appropriate length, approximately 50cm (20in). Try not to damage the bark on the trunk, as this helps to retain the moisture.

MUSHROOMS

Italian oyster (*Pleurotus pulmonarius*)
Nameko (*Pholiota microspora*)
Shiitake (*Lentinula edodes*)*

*A specific strain of shiitake mushroom spawn will need to be sourced for this, so always consult your supplier before ordering, to make sure their dowels will suit your tree of choice.

MATERIALS

• Fir (*Abies*) Christmas tree
• Saw or secateurs
• 20-30 freshly inoculated dowels, kept refrigerated until needed
• Drill and drill bit, to match size of the dowels
• Alcohol sanitizer wipes or spray, or boiling water
• Pen or tape
• Hammer
• 50g (2oz) good-quality bees- or soy wax
• Heat source to melt your wax
• Soft sponge dabber or a paintbrush, to apply the melted wax
• Watering can or hose (optional)

Once cut, position a protective layer under the log – this is to shield the surface below from any dripping wax.

Inoculating the log

Remove your dowels from the fridge and leave to acclimatize. Clean your drill bit with sanitizer or boiling water. Using a pen or tape, mark the length of your dowels on the drill bit – this will ensure your holes are the same depth as your dowels are long. They should sit flush with the surface of your log once inserted.

Mark your first row for the dowels along the length of your log, with eight evenly spaced points. For the next row, offset seven evenly spaced points from the first row. For thirty dowels, you will need to mark four alternating rows altogether, which will give you a diamond configuration around your log and ensure even colonization of the mycelium.

Drill your holes where marked, to the depth of your pen mark or tape. Place a dowel into a hole and hammer it in until it is flush with the surface of the log. Do this for all thirty dowels.

Warm the wax until it has all melted and leave it over a low heat. Use your sponge dabber or paintbrush to apply the melted wax over the dowels and any cut branches to seal them. Sealing helps to protect your dowels from squirrels and insects during the incubation period. Do not seal the two cut ends of your log: these should be left open to allow for water absorption.

Mark your log so that it can be readily identified. You need to be able to identify the mushrooms growing from your log, too. Then place your log in your chosen spot, either lying it down or leaning it upright. A covering of leaf mulch will help protect it from the elements.

Keep checking on your log throughout the months for signs of fruiting and to make sure it isn't drying out. If there is no rainfall for a week, or if your log is sheltered from the rain, remember to sprinkle it weekly with a watering can or hose.

Harvesting your mushrooms

Your log will begin to fruit about 10–12 months after being inoculated. Nameko mushrooms like to fruit in cold temperatures, so keep an eye on your log when the temperatures drop and after heavy rainfall. Italian oyster mushrooms and shiitake can fruit a little earlier in the year. When growing outdoors there is always a risk of wild spores from other fungi colonizing your log, so clear confident identification is essential. Make sure to check the caps, gills and stems for similarities or variants before picking.

We recommend harvesting your mushrooms when they are still young, to ensure they are fresh and delicious. To do this, pinch each mushroom at its base, close to the log, and twist. Alternatively, you can cut your mushrooms off with a knife or scissors.

You may find you get several flushes of mushrooms over the fruiting season.

TIP To give your project the very best chance, you will need freshly inoculated dowels. If you're planning to make the most of an unwanted Christmas tree, order your dowels before Christmas and pop them in your fridge ready to grow as soon as a tree becomes available.

Mushroom Tincture

How to get the most out of your mushrooms

By making a tincture, you extract the maximum nutritional value from your mushrooms. Being another cupboard staple, tinctures provide the perfect way to receive a daily dose of this incredibly nourishing foodstuff.

You can follow the whole of this project for the double extraction tincture method, or simply focus on one of the stages detailed below.

The first stage uses alcohol to draw out all the non-water-soluble compounds from your dried mushrooms. It is a great product to use on less easily digested medicinal mushroom such as reishi and turkey tail.

The second stage is a decoction technique, which uses heat and water to extract the mushroom essence. This works well with other edible mushrooms and draws out water-soluble compounds that are well known for their anti-inflammatory and antioxidant properties.

Double extraction – using both stages described above – will provide the best tinctures and is well worth the extra efforts, but both approaches have their merits.

WHEN This project can be started at any time of the year. You'll need to steep your mushrooms for 2–8 weeks in the first stage of preparation.

WHERE The first stage (using alcohol) is a simple mix-and-soak task. You will then need to leave your mixture to infuse in a dark, cool cupboard, shaking the contents daily.

MUSHROOMS

Use any dried or fresh edible mushroom from the Mushroom Directory (see pages 160–84).

ALCOHOL STAGE MATERIALS

• 30g (1oz) dried mushrooms, coarsely chopped
• 500ml (17½fl. oz) glass Mason jar or glass bottle with a wide opening
• 250ml (9fl. oz) good-quality vodka, min. 40 per cent alcohol by volume
• Baking paper
• Fine muslin cloth, to cover 1sq. m (11sq. ft)
• Bowl
• Funnel, for decanting your tincture
• 100ml (3½fl. oz) glass dropper bottle
• Self-adhesive labels
• Pen

DECOCTION STAGE MATERIALS

• 500ml (17½fl. oz) spring or filtered water
• Saucepan
• Hob or gas stove
• Funnel, for decanting your decoction mixture
• Fine muslin cloth, to cover 1sq. m (11sq. ft)
• Bowl
• 100ml (3½fl. oz) glass dropper bottle
• Self-adhesive labels and pen, for labelling

Method

Alcohol stage

Add your dried mushrooms to the Mason jar. Fill it halfway with the vodka, making sure that the mushrooms are completely covered. Place the baking paper between the jar and its lid before closing; then shake well.

Store the jar in a cool dark cupboard, and give it a shake every day. The longer you leave your mushrooms to infuse, the stronger your tincture will be.

When you are ready to bottle your infusion, take your bowl and cover it with the muslin. Strain your mixture through the muslin, reserving the liquid and the mushrooms. Double your muslin cloth to catch the finer mushrooms within the liquid. Decant the liquid back into your Mason jar and close with the baking paper in place.

If you're stopping at this stage, use the funnel to decant some of your tincture into your dropper bottle and store it and the jar for up to a year in a cool dark cupboard. Don't forget to date and label both containers.

Decoction stage

Add the strained mushrooms and the water to a saucepan. Bring the mixture to the boil and simmer on a very low heat for two hours. Keep topping up the mixture with water, if necessary, to ensure it doesn't boil dry.

Once your mixture has reduced by half and has a thicker, mud-like consistency, remove the saucepan from the heat, cover it and leave the mixture to cool completely. Strain your mixture into a bowl through the muslin, reserving the mushroom-infused water and disposing of the mushrooms.

Final tasks

If completing both stages, combine the mushroom-infused water with the alcohol extract inside your Mason jar. Then use the funnel to decant your combined tincture into your dropper bottle. Label both your jar and bottle with your mushroom ingredients and the date you mixed both the alcohol and water extracts together.

Taking your tincture

The dropper bottle allows you to monitor your daily dosage, which you can vary depending on your requirements. It's recommended that you take between one-third and a full dropper each day. This dosage can be spread out over the course of the day or taken in one go. We don't recommend exceeding a full dropper of tincture (approx. 2ml).

TIP The water-based tincture alone won't last as long as the alcohol-based one, so keep it chilled and use within one month.

Dried Mushrooms

A mushroom-lover's must-have

Drying is one of the best ways to preserve and store all types of mushrooms. As they dry, the mushrooms' flavours and aromas intensify, becoming deep and delicately earthy and highlighting the unique umami flavours that they are well known for.

WHEN In this project we explore three different drying techniques. The first is natural drying, which gives its best results during the warmer and longer days of summer and early autumn. The other two techniques (air and oven drying) can be used year-round.

WHERE Natural drying will need fresh air and the warmth of the sun over the course of a few days. Air and oven drying can be done in your kitchen.

MUSHROOMS

Any dried or fresh edible mushroom from the Mushroom Directory (see pages 160–84).

MATERIALS

- 250g (9oz) fresh mushrooms
- Knife (optional)
- Airtight container, for storing your dried mushrooms
- Self-adhesive label
- Pen
- Heatproof bowl
- Boiling water

FOR NATURAL DRYING

- Large shallow bowl

FOR OVEN DRYING

- Oven
- Baking tray
- Baking paper

FOR AIR DRYING

- Dehumidifier

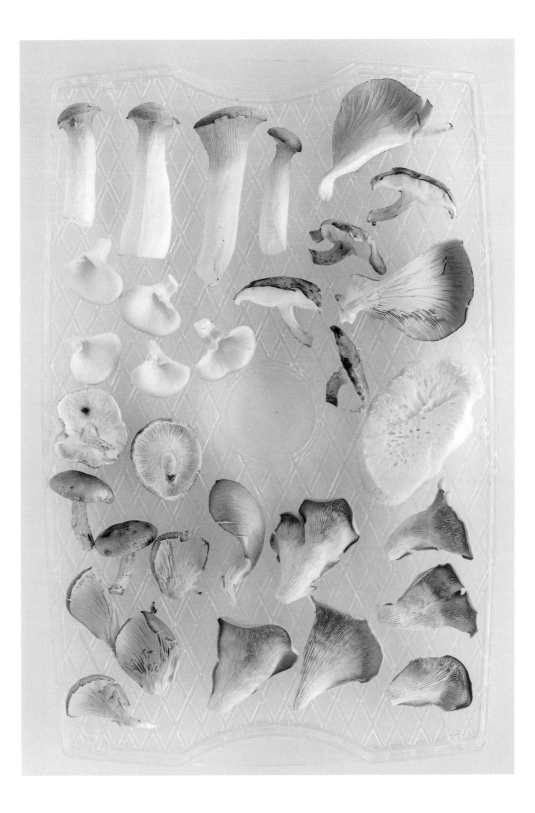

Method

Natural drying

Tear or slice your mushroom into even segments. If you're drying small or thin mushrooms, you may want to keep these whole.

Arrange your mushrooms with their gills facing up in your large shallow bowl. Place the bowl in the sun or in a warm and dry environment with plenty of airflow.

After six hours, turn your mushrooms; repeat this step until your mushrooms are completely dry.

Oven drying

Preheat your oven to 70°C (150°F; gas mark ½) and line your baking tray with baking paper.

Evenly slice your mushrooms and arrange them evenly on the baking paper, making sure you leave space between each slice. Place your baking tray in the oven and leave for about three hours. Check on your mushrooms every hour. By opening the door, you will release the moisture within the oven and assist the drying process. Remove trays from the oven when your mushrooms are cracker dry, nice and crisp to the touch.

Storing and rehydrating your mushrooms

Label and store your mushrooms in an airtight container in a cool dry environment. In such conditions, they can keep for up to a year.

When you're ready to eat your mushrooms, you can rehydrate them by placing them in a heatproof bowl and covering with boiling water. Soak the mushrooms for 20–30 minutes to soften, before using. Alternatively, you can turn the dried mushrooms into a mushroom powder (see page 154).

TIP Notice how your mushrooms change throughout the drying process. They will begin to appear wrinkly, then become rubbery to the touch. Eventually, they will be cracker dry and crispy. Sun-drying your mushrooms will also supercharge your mushrooms with vitamin D (see our Vitamin D Boost project, page 144).

Vitamin D Boost
Supercharge your mushrooms with vitamin D

Much like us, mushrooms can transform ultraviolet light from the sun into vitamin D, which is an essential immune-boosting substance that also helps us to absorb calcium, strengthening our teeth and bones. However, because vitamin D is largely produced when our skin is exposed to the sun, we need to source it elsewhere during the cooler darker months of winter. That's where mushrooms come to the rescue.

If you place your home-grown mushrooms on an open windowsill or outdoors in the sun, they will begin to absorb and convert the sunlight into high levels of vitamin D. What's more, they stay charged, too, even after being dried, cooked or placed in the fridge. By contrast, many shop-brought mushrooms are grown in the dark or under electric lighting and have relatively low levels of it.

WHEN Midday sunlight between early summer and early autumn will expose your mushrooms to the best of the sun. But regardless of the time of year or day, sunlight can add value to your home-grown mushrooms.

WHERE Somewhere in full sun. Choose a spot outdoors or by an open window, because glass windowpanes and plastic coverings do not allow sufficient levels of ultraviolet light to penetrate, for the mushrooms to reap the rewards.

Method

Getting started
Arrange your mushrooms with their gills facing up in your bowl. Leave the bowl in full sun for 15–120 minutes. This sunlight exposure can be achieved over the course of a few days. The longer your mushrooms are left to sun-dry, the more vitamin D they will absorb and retain.

MUSHROOMS

Any edible mushroom such as:
- Button (*Agaricus bisporus var. bisporus*)
- Oyster (*Pleurotus spp.*)
- Portobello (*Agaricus bisporus*)
- Shiitake (*Lentinula edodes*)
- White cremini (*Agaricus bisporus var. bisporus*)

MATERIALS
- Mushrooms shop-brought or home-grown
- Large shallow bowl

TIP Sun-drying your mushrooms not only supercharges them with vitamin D, but also preserves them beautifully (see also Dried Mushrooms, page 134). Any edible mushroom will benefit from exposure to the sun, but, if you're looking to maximize your intake, the shiitake is the supercharger, gaining and retaining the most vitamin D.

Mushroom Coffee

Kickstart your day with a cold-brew, mushroom-infused coffee

Why not extract the goodness from your favourite coffee and mushrooms for a refreshingly chilled brew?

Dried mushrooms have a deep and intense flavour that infuses beautifully when stewed in boiling water. When combined with the cold-brew process, you can extract all the qualities you seek in a delicious coffee. The chilled technique brings out the smoother and less acidic flavours of the coffee beans while harnessing the goodness and earthy tones of your dried mushrooms.

WHEN You will need 18–24 hours to prepare your coffee. Once brewed, it will last up to 48 hours in the fridge.

WHERE A kitchen setting or wherever you usually make your morning cuppa.

MUSHROOMS

Any dried edible mushrooms listed within the Mushroom Directory (see pages 160–84).

See also Dried Mushrooms (page 134) for details on how to dry your own mushrooms

MATERIALS

- Heatproof bowl
- 20g (¾oz) dried mushrooms
- 500ml (17½fl. oz) boiling filtered water
- Spoon
- 1 tsp honey (optional)
- 50g (2oz) coarsely ground coffee
- Sieve
- Kitchen paper
- Measuring jug
- 500ml (17½fl. oz) glass jar or bottle with lid

Method

Getting started

The ingredients and instructions below are a guide – you can adjust the concentrations of coffee and mushrooms to suit your tastes. Just avoid finely ground coffee as it could over-infuse, and it is harder to strain.

In the bowl, soak your mushrooms in the boiled water and leave to cool completely. If you have a sweet tooth, dissolve a teaspoon of honey into the liquid while infusing your mushrooms.

After about half an hour, use the sieve to strain the mushrooms, reserving the mushroom-infused water. Then discard the mushrooms. Add the coffee grounds to the mushroom-infused water, using the spoon, and lightly mix. Cover and leave to rest – do not stir.

After 12–15 hours, strain the mixture through the sieve lined with kitchen paper. Use the jug to decant the mushroom–coffee infusion into your glass jar or bottle.

Serve the mushroom coffee

Dilute one part mushroom–coffee infusion to one part chilled water or milk to make the mushroom coffee; or serve it neat over ice.

If you'd like a warm infusion, simply heat the mushroom coffee in the microwave.

TIP Instead of discarding them, why not add your soaked mushrooms to a soup or stew. They will keep in the fridge for up to three days, or you can freeze them for use later.

1

4

Mushroom Infusions

Extracting the goodness to create a warm hug in a mug

This project is a great way to use your glorious home-dried mushrooms (see page 134) or those you have stored in your cupboard. By steeping the dried mushrooms in hot water, you can extract their delicious earthy flavours and unlock their nutritional goodness. We like to add a touch of miso to enhance that umami flavour.

WHEN Your infusion will take only a few minutes to make. It can be chilled and will last a couple of days in the fridge.

WHERE A kitchen setting or wherever you usually make your midday brew (see pages 162–185).

Method

Getting started

The ingredients and instructions here are a guide – you can adjust the strength of your infusion by increasing or reducing the quantities of mushrooms, miso and/or stewing time to suit your tastes.

Place your dried mushrooms inside your teapot or jug, then add your boiling water. Stir in the miso paste until dissolved. Leave to stew for at least five minutes, and then serve. You can discard the mushrooms or save them to use elsewhere.

To chill

Leave your infusion to cool completely. Decant through the tea strainer into a lidded glass jar or bottle and store in the fridge for up to 48 hours. Your chilled mushroom infusion is a welcome cooler on hot days, especially if served over ice with a slice of lemon.

MUSHROOMS

Any dried edible mushrooms from the Mushroom Directory (see pages 160–84).

MATERIALS

(for two people)

• 10–15g (½oz) whole dried mushrooms
• Teapot or jug
• 500ml (17½fl. oz) boiling filtered water
• ½ level tsp miso paste
• Spoon

FOR CHILLING

• Tea strainer
• Lidded glass jar or bottle

TIP You can swap the miso paste for a teaspoon of honey for a sweeter brew.

Mushroom Seasoning

Adding that umami flavour and nutrition to any dish

Here, we've put together a simple recipe for turning your dried mushrooms into an intensely delicious seasoning, packed with umami tones. We recommend using this great addition to your pantry as a complementary seasoning that adds depth and a rich savoury flavour to any dish.

Use a food blender or spice grinder for a fine blend. Alternatively, a pestle and mortar will give your seasoning a coarser texture that works well with the other ingredients here.

Method

Getting started

Add your mushrooms to your food blender, spice grinder or pestle and mortar, and grind to your desired texture. Add your herbs and blend again – a shorter blend will give you a courser texture.

Transfer to a jar and stir in your salt. Your seasoning mix will keep well for six months in an airtight container.

TIP You can use any herbs that are at the end of their fresh shelf life. For additional flavour twists, try adding pepper, dried garlic powder or onion powder. Consider a smoked spicy hit, too, of smoked dried garlic or smoked paprika and chilli flakes.

MUSHROOMS

Dried king oyster (*Pleurotus eryngii*)
Dried lion's mane (*Hericium erinaceus*)
Dried pink oyster (*Pleurotus djamor*)
Dried shiitake (*Lentinula edodes*)

INGREDIENTS*

• 30g (1oz) dried mushrooms – you can use one type or a mixture
• 1 tsp dried sage (*Salvia officinalis*), finely chopped or ground
• 1 tsp dried rosemary (*Salvia rosmarinus*), finely chopped or ground
• ½ tsp dried thyme (*Thymus vulgaris*), finely ground or chopped
• 60g (2oz) good-quality sea salt crystals or flakes

EQUIPMENT

• Food blender or spice grinder, or pestle and mortar
• Storage jar

* We recommend using no more than three different herbs, which you can adjust to your taste and availability. Here we have chosen sage, rosemary and thyme.

Mushroom Powder
Harnessing the power of mushrooms

By turning your dried mushrooms into a powder, it is particularly easy to enjoy their nutritional goodness. Mushroom powder is a beautifully versatile ingredient that can be added to homemade granolas, marinades, soups and stews. You can also use it in bread, cake and brownie mixtures, as well as your daily smoothies and cafetière for that extra morning boost.

By combining a variety of mushrooms in your powder, you will benefit from their multiple super health-boosting qualities and flavour-packed properties in one hit.

WHEN Whenever you have a surplus of dried mushrooms! See our project on drying mushrooms (page 140) if you have lots of fresh mushrooms to hand.

WHERE Your kitchen.

MUSHROOMS

Any dried or fresh edible mushroom from the Mushroom Directory (see pages 160–84).

MATERIALS

• Dried mushrooms, min. 30g (1oz) or 250g (9oz) fresh edible mushrooms
• Food blender or spice grinder
• Glass storage jar
• Self-adhesive label
• Pen

Method

Getting started
Place your dried mushrooms in your blender or spice grinder, and process into a fine powder. Pour your powder into an airtight jar and label it with the mushroom mix details and the date. Store the mushroom powder in a cool dark cupboard; it will keep for up to a year.

TIP For a nutritional boost, you can swap up to 20g (¾oz) flour for the same quantity of mushroom powder in a brownie recipe and also in bread. See also Mushroom Seasoning (page 152), Mushroom Tinctures (page 136) and Mushroom Coffee (page 146) for other ideas on how to use mushroom powder.

Pickled Mushrooms

Preserving your mushrooms

An old recipe has been resurrected for a modern generation keen on zero waste. Its simple pickling technique preserves your mushrooms by steeping them in brine. At the same time, the mushrooms maintain both their firm texture and fresh taste. The longer you leave the pickled mushrooms in the fridge, the more your mushrooms will absorb flavours from the herbs.

Such pickled mushrooms are a great addition to any charcuterie board or salad dish, and also make a great homemade gift guaranteed to wow your friends. *Bon appétit.*

MUSHROOMS

Button (*Agaricus bisporus* var. *bisporus*)
Cremini (*Agaricus bisporus* var. *bisporus*)
Oyster (*Pleurotus spp.*)
Shiitake (*Lentinula edodes*)

INGREDIENTS

- 150ml (5fl. oz) water
- 150ml (5fl. oz) white wine vinegar or apple cider vinegar
- 2 level tsp sea salt
- 4 level tsp sugar
- 1 tsp Dijon mustard
- 225g (8oz) mushrooms
- 2 shallots
- 1 heaped tbsp of mixed fresh, finely chopped herbs such as dill (*Anethum graveolens*), rosemary (*Salvia rosmarinus*) and tarragon (*Artemisia dracunculus*)

EQUIPMENT

- 500ml (16oz) Mason jar or lidded glass jar
- Baking tray
- Saucepan
- Wooden spoon
- Knife
- Chopping board
- Bowl

Method

Getting started

Sterilize your jar by washing it in soapy water and then placing the jar upside down on a baking tray (remove the rubber if you are using a Mason jar). Place the jar in an oven heated to 140°C Fan/160°C/320°F/gas mark 3 for 10 minutes. Leave to cool. Alternatively, you can wash it in a dishwasher at maximum temperature.

Put your water, vinegar, salt and sugar in the saucepan, bring to a boil then take the mixture off the heat immediately. Add the Dijon mustard, stirring with the wooden spoon until dissolved – this is your pickling liquor.

Cut any large mushrooms into 2mm (⅟₁₂in) slices – this will help them remain firm in texture – and finely chop your shallots. Mix all your fresh ingredients in the bowl and add them to the jar. Fresh oyster mushrooms will fill your jars more easily as they're less dense and more malleable. Sliced cremini and shiitake mushrooms are firmer, so you may need fewer to fill your jar.

Pour your warm pickling liquor into the jar until the mushrooms are covered. Seal the jar with its lid and allow the mixture to cool.

After two hours, move your jar into the fridge and store for twenty-four hours before eating. Your pickled mushrooms will keep for one month unopened. Be sure to consume within three days of opening the jar.

Serving ideas

Your pickled mushrooms will go well with cheese, pâté or sliced avocado, covered with a drizzle of olive oil and served on a savoury cracker or freshly toasted bread. Too good.

TIP As well as using any herbs you might already have in the fridge or growing in the garden, consider adding other vegetables to the fresh ingredients mixture, such as a thinly sliced carrot or small cauliflower florets. A pinch of fennel and a slice or two of red chilli also provide delicious flavours.

Part 3

Mushroom Directory

Mushrooms for Growing Indoors

There is an abundance of mushrooms that will happily grow indoors under a watchful eye. What's more, mushrooms can be grown indoors year-round, sitting happily among your houseplants. Regardless of the type and amount of space you have, there will be a mushroom project for you (see pages 42–159).

Most mushrooms listed here for indoor growing (see pages 160–9) need light and frequent watering to get growing. Other than that, they are very low-maintenance. You can read more about starting your growing journey in Basic Mushroom Care (see pages 26–7).

One of the greatest advantages of growing indoors is what we like to call 'kitchen foraging', and allows you to harvest delicious mushroom without fear of misidentifying your crop, and without the risk of insects feasting on your crop before you do. Happy growing!

Portobello mushrooms

Agaricus bisporus

These large, white- or brown-capped mushrooms, which are also known as portabella mushrooms, can be easily identified by their thick, flat caps and short, white stem. Wild portobello mushrooms can be found popping up in grasslands across Europe and North America, and are also commercially cultivated worldwide.

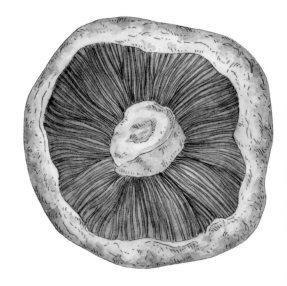

Portobello mushrooms are harvested once they reach their full size and after their caps have flattened out, exposing the dark brown or pink gills underneath. If harvested earlier than this, portobello mushrooms are known as button, white or cremini mushrooms (see page 163).

Portobello mushrooms like to grow in the dark on sterilised, nutrient-rich or manure-based composts. Using a layer of damp newspapers to keep the surface moist and environment dark, they can be grown indoors or outdoors in temperatures of 18–23°C (64–73°F).

Portobello mushrooms have a rich meaty texture, and are often stuffed, marinated and baked.

Button, white or cremini mushrooms

Agaricus bisporus var. *bisporus*

The common and familiar, white, closed-capped, button or cremini mushroom belong to the same species as the portobello mushrooms (see page 162) but harvested at different stages of growth – the button or 'baby' mushrooms being harvested the earliest.

During autumn, they are to be found growing in grasslands, fields and meadows across Europe and North America. They are also cultivated worldwide on racked trays of rich compost in large dark warehouses.

These white-coloured mushrooms don't require any light and can be grown in boxes at home at any time of year. One of the first grow-at-home-mushrooms kits, produced in the 1980s, used this species; they featured a polystyrene box that could live in your cellar or kitchen cupboard.

A brown-capped variation of the white mushroom is the common brown mushroom, often referred to in supermarkets as 'chestnut mushrooms'. In cultivation, these chestnut mushrooms are more often exposed to ultraviolet light after they have been harvested, giving them the vitamin D boost they are so well known for (see Common Misconceptions, page 17.)

Button, white, cremini and brown-capped mushrooms are very versatile and have a classic but mild mushroom flavour – we love them fried and served on toast with plenty of butter.

Cordyceps mushrooms

Cordyceps militaris

This parasitic fungus, which is also known as the scarlet caterpillar mushroom, inhabits the bodies of live insects. It infects, consumes and mummifies the host before fruiting a single, club shaped mushroom.

Not being a traditional cap and-stem fungus, the cordyceps gets its name from *cord* (meaning club) and *ceps* (meaning head). It has a bright red or orange fruiting body, and is native to Asia.

However, cordyceps is also commercially cultivated on more vegan-friendly substrate, such as brown rice.

Cordyceps is noted to have a mild mushroom flavour with sweet honey notes and can be used fresh or dried in cooking. It is used in traditional Chinese herbalism steeped in tea and is now commonly made into powders.

Enoki mushrooms

Flammulina filiformis

When grown indoors in the dark, these mushrooms, also known as enokitake, take on an almost noodle-like form, with long, thin, white stems and small, gilled caps, which grow tall looking for the light. Ranging from pale yellow to almost white, enoki mushrooms are known for their sweet flavour.

Traditionally cultivated in East Asia, enoki can be grown in plastic bags or glass jars on a substrate of hardwood sawdust, straw and even books. They can also be grown on hardwood logs outdoors, including pine (*Pinus*) – but you will find they take on a remarkably different appearance in this instance, sporting a darker colour and larger caps.

These mushrooms must be cooked and should not be eaten raw. They are mild in flavour and have a unique crunch, even when cooked. Enoki mushrooms go well in broths, soups and stir-fries.

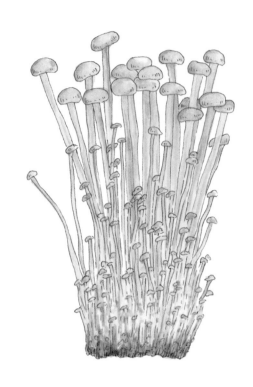

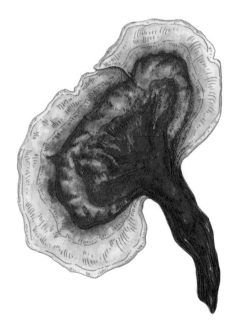

Reishi mushrooms

Ganoderma lingzhi

Reishi has shiny surface and dark colouring, with a pitted underside. When home growing, if you increase the level of CO_2 within their growing environment, you can encourage them to develop a delicate, sculptural 'reishi antlers', coral-like forms that reach up towards the fresh air as they grow.

In the wild, reishi take on a more kidney-like form and can be found growing on the side of dead or decaying trees and are native to the East Asia region. For indoor cultivation, they love warmth and will thrive in a sunny room or greenhouse when grown on a sawdust-supplemented substrate. They can also be cultivated outdoors on hardwood logs in more temperate climates.

Reishi mushrooms are not traditionally used in cooking, but they can be dried and made into teas and tinctures (see Mushroom Tincture, page 130).

Lion's mane mushrooms

Hericium erinaceus

Also known as a tooth fungus, this mushroom has a stunning, mane-like appearance. It's usually found growing in single clumps, and thrives on damp and decaying hardwoods such as oak and beech. Although native to North America, Asia and Europe, here in the UK it is so rare growing in the wild that it has been designated a protected species and is illegal to forage.

Lucky for us, it is an easy mushroom to cultivate and will happily grow indoors on a hardwood sawdust substrate or outdoors on inoculated hardwood logs.

It has an almost crabmeat texture, as well as a delicate aroma that intensifies when griddled or dried. Lion's mane is also porous, so perfect for marinating and popping on the barbecue.

Shiitake

Lentinula edodes

In Japanese, *shii* translates as 'tree' and *take* as 'mushroom'. In the wild, shiitake are found growing on dead and decaying deciduous trees like oak, chestnut (*Castanea* and *Aesculus*), maple (*Acer*) and beech, and they enjoy warm, moist climates.

Shiitake can be grown indoors on hardwood sawdust, grain and used coffee grounds. As the incubation process comes to an end, your substrate block will begin to turn brown. This dark brown outer layer forms a protective crust over the substrate.

These mushrooms can also be grown outdoors on hardwood logs (see page 86). By growing outdoors, you can harvest fresh mushrooms throughout the year.

The process of cold-water shocking will force regular fruiting. Shiitake are delicious when eaten fresh, and they preserve well when dried. They have a strong and deep umami mushroom flavour that can enhance broths and stocks.

Chestnut mushrooms

Pholiota adiposa

This delicious gourmet mushroom is not the same as the common brown mushroom found in local supermarkets (see page 163). These chestnut mushrooms have a textured cap and a slightly shaggy appearance, with pale yellow gills and a scaly stem. They can be cultivated indoors on mixed substrates, and in the wild can be found growing on dead or dying beech trees.

Chestnut mushrooms have many non-edible – some even deadly – lookalikes that grow in similar conditions outdoors. You can also grow them outdoors on oak logs (see page 86), but make sure to correctly identify them once ready to harvest.

These mushrooms have a mild and nutty flavour and remain firm when cooked.

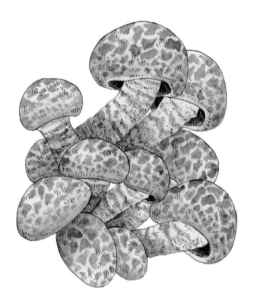

Yellow oyster mushrooms

Pleurotus citrinopileatus

Also known as the golden oyster mushroom, these brightly coloured mushrooms grow in dense clusters and have smaller, more tubular caps than their grey and pink 'siblings'.

Although native to Asia, yellow oyster mushrooms can now be found growing across the globe, popping up in early spring and late autumn when the weather is milder and more humid.

They love to grow on hardwoods but can be cultivated on other substrates such as sawdust, straw, soyhulls and other materials such as books and denim.

Yellow oyster mushrooms have a creamy, delicate flavour, similar to that of the cashew nut – they are a visual and tasty asset to any pasta or salad dish.

Pink oyster mushrooms

Pleurotus djamor

These vibrant pink mushrooms are curvaceous and delicate, appearing petal-like when fully formed. They typically like warmer weather and can be found growing on hardwoods in tropical climates. Indoors, they can be grown on substrates such as coffee grounds, straw and sawdust, in temperatures of at least 18°C (64°F).

Once pink oyster mushrooms start growing, they develop quickly and are ready to harvest in a very short space of time. They have a unique flavour often described as 'meaty', or sometimes reminiscent of seafood. They crisp up nicely when dry fried and are a fantastic addition to a simple risotto.

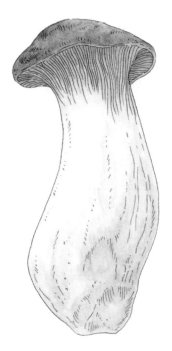

King oyster mushrooms

Pleurotus eryngii

With their standout chunky stems and small-gilled caps, king oyster mushrooms are easily recognizable. Although notoriously difficult to grow, their unique texture and flavour are well worth the extra effort.

King oyster mushrooms are native to southern Europe, North Africa, central Asia and Russia, where traditionally they are found growing from the roots of hardwood trees, popping up through the undergrowth. Indoors, they can be grown in ceramic jars or plastic grow bags on a hardwood sawdust-supplemented substrate.

The dense stems of king oyster mushroom can be torn to resemble shredded chicken or be sliced into discs and sautéed to imitate seared scallops; they have a rich umami flavour. Being a versatile mushroom packed with protein, they make a great meat substitute.

Grey oyster mushrooms

Pleurotus ostreatus

The form of this delicate, gilled mushroom is often likened to that of an oyster shell. In the wild, grey oyster mushrooms are commonly found growing on the side of dead trees from mid-autumn through to the first frosts in temperate and tropical climates.

They are a hardy, versatile mushroom that can be grown outdoors or indoors year-round, on a variety of readily available substrates, from coffee grounds to straw, books and clothing. They have a mild and familiar 'mushroom-like' flavour and can been eaten raw or cooked; they're delicious on their own, but also form a great pairing with stronger flavours.

Black pearl oyster mushrooms

Pleurotus ostreatus × *P. eryngii*

The black pearl oyster mushroom is a hybrid of the easy-to-grow grey oyster mushroom and stocky-stemmed king oyster mushroom. Their darker caps and thicker stems resemble the king oyster mushroom, but they grow slightly slimmer and in clusters like the grey oyster mushroom.

Black pearl oyster mushrooms can be grown indoors on a hardwood sawdust-based substrate, or on hardwood logs like oak, using the dowel method (see page 86).

They have the savoury and earthy flavour of the classic oyster mushroom but with a hearty texture similar to that of the king oyster. They are ideal for broths or meat dishes or as a meat substitute.

Straw mushrooms

Volvariella volvacea

In east and south-east Asia, where they are native, straw mushrooms are traditionally picked when young and while their caps are still closed. They thrive in humid, subtropical environments, and can be ready to harvest within just a week of pinning if temperatures hover around 27°C (80°F). Straw mushrooms are renowned for being easy to cultivate. Their name is derived from the straw they grow on, and they are cultivated heavily in China on rice straw, but they will also develop on cotton and wheat straw.

Straw mushrooms are a great source of protein, and they are often preserved in jars or tins. Their mild, earthy flavour is particularly delicious when fried with a bit of garlic butter, served with noodles or added to soups.

Mushrooms for Growing Outdoors

In this section we explore a variety of mushrooms that can be grown in your outdoor space, regardless of its size, orientation or soil type. Introducing fungi into your garden, balcony or allotment brings many benefits, such as improving the health of your soil and increasing the diversity of your local wildlife.

As ever, we encourage you to properly identify any mushroom you hope to harvest by their caps, stems, spores and flesh (see pages 32–3). Outdoors, there is always the chance of another mushroom capitalizing on the lovely environment you have created for your own crop, so do make sure that what you are harvesting is the mushroom you had intended to grow. If you are trying any new fungi, make sure it is an edible variety and fully cooked, then sample a very small bit of it to ensure you have no adverse reaction. If all is well, you can then enjoy the rest of your harvest.

Crown-tipped coral mushrooms

Artomyces pyxidatus

Easily identified by its small, crown-like form at the tip, this particular coral mushroom is a fragile variety mostly found growing on decaying vegetation or timber at ground level. Named for its coral-like appearance, the crown-tipped coral mushroom's multiple thin branches grow upwards in a pale cream to light brown colour, turning slightly pink as they mature.

The best time to harvest this coral mushroom is early summer through to autumn. It can be found growing on buried beech wood, woodchips and mulch in temperate climates.

Its mild aroma and delicate, earthy flavour suit its use as a garnish; it can also be battered, fried or pickled. Similar-looking mushrooms but brighter coloured can be harmful if ingested, so take care to identify crown-tipped coral mushrooms correctly when harvesting.

Shaggy mane mushrooms

Coprinus comatus

A very common and delicate wild mushroom, named after the 'shaggy' appearance of its conical shaped caps. Pale grey or off-white in colour, Shaggy mane mushrooms are best harvested while young, when the caps are closed and gills still white. As they reach maturity the gills turn black and the mushrooms become inky and bitter in taste.

Shaggy manes are often found growing in grasslands and at the edges of sports fields in late summer and into autumn. They can be grown outdoors in mushroom beds on coco coir or straw and manure.

Best picked when young, they'll begin to perish soon after being harvested, but can be frozen for preservation. See Mushroom Ink (page 60) for ideas on how you can use this precious mushroom as ink.

Beefsteak mushrooms

Fistulina hepatica

This unusual bracket mushroom gets its name from its appearance: with its red and sticky-looking surface, it can look like a tongue growing out of the side of a tree when young, or like a raw beef steak as it matures. It even appears to bleed when cut.

The beefsteak mushroom is suitable for growing on large logs as it thrives on the more plentiful supply of nutrients. We recommend growing on oak and sweet chestnut logs using the dowel method (see page 86). It will fruit from late summer to late autumn in temperate climates and is best harvested when young; its appearance darkens with age.

The slightly sour, acidic taste is not to everyone's liking, but beefsteak mushrooms can be delicious if marinaded overnight before cooking.

Velvet shank mushrooms

Flammulina velutipes

Velvet shanks are one of a few winter mushrooms that appear after the first frosts or snowfall, and which can be found growing through spring. They grow on dead and decaying hardwood, deciduous trees, such as beech, elm (*Ulmus*), ash (*Fraxinus*) and oak, and can be grown at home on many hardwood timbers (see page 86).

When growing outdoors, velvet shank mushrooms are usually orange, yellow or pale brown in colour – often darker in the middle – with white gills and a velvety stem that goes from pale to dark. They have a similar appearance to the deadly skullcap but are found growing in different seasons. When grown indoors they take on a very difference appearance with longer stems and can be paler in colour.

Velvet shank mushrooms, which are sweet in flavour, make a delicious soup. They should always be cooked before eating; the stems can be tough and are best discarded.

Maitake

Grifola frondosa

Also known as hen of the woods, maitake is a polypore bracket fungus so doesn't have gills as is traditionally associated with more common mushrooms. It is a perennial fungus that fruits from late autumn until mid-winter, and can be found growing at the bottom of tree stumps and on the roots of trees. Although native to China, it also thrives on oak, maple and elm trees in temperate climates. You can grow maitake outdoors on freshly felled and inoculated hardwood logs (see page 120).

It is best harvested when young and tender, and has a frilly appearance, with an earthy and slightly peppery flavour when cooked.

Chicken of the woods mushrooms

Laetiporus sulphureus

This stunning bracket fungus has a bright orange to golden yellow colouring. It can be found growing on tree trunks and branches in a shelf-like form from late spring through to late summer. If harvested from the wild, make sure to identify the specific tree type – gums (*Eucalyptus*) as well as yews (*Taxus*) and other conifers contain tree oils that can be absorbed by the mushrooms and which can cause serious digestive issues.

Fortunately, chicken of the woods can be grown on oak, cherry (*Prunus*), sweet chestnut and ash (see page 86) or on stacked hardwood discs (see page 120). You will need a shady spot and regular watering.

This mushroom derives its name from its texture and taste, and is best harvested when young, when its soft sponginess most resembles chicken. It must be cooked before being eaten: stir-fry, marinade or cook as part of a stew.

True morel mushrooms

Morchella esculenta

An early-fruiting fungi, the true or common morel can be found popping up in woodlands and pastures across Europe including the UK. It's very distinct, with a dark, honeycomb-textured cap and hollow white stem.

The true morel mushroom appears in early spring, once temperatures start to warm up but the weather is still damp with cool nights. Renowned for being difficult to cultivate, the true morel can be grown on a bed of firepit ash (see page 124).

This prized and sought-after mushroom must be cooked thoroughly. It has a delicate, flavour with a strong, earthy aroma. Not to be mistaken for the false morel, which can be toxic, or even deadly if over consumed.

Nameko mushrooms

Pholiota microspora

Ranging from orange to amber in colour, the nameko mushroom is characterized by its delicate gills, straight stem and glossy, wet-look cap. They're commonly found growing in the temperate highlands of northern Asia.

Using the dowel method (see page 86), the nameko can be grown on bundles of thin logs or branches; help keep the logs damp by storing them under a layer of leaf litter. The mushrooms will fruit after temperatures drop in autumn, and continue through to early winter. You can use softwood to grow these mushrooms (see page 132).

Nameko mushrooms are a key ingredient in miso soup. They have an earthy, cashew-like flavour and maintain their crunch and texture once cooked. They can also be dried.

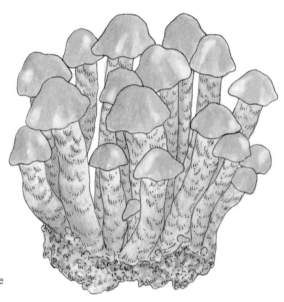

White oyster mushrooms

Pleurotus cornucopiae

The glorious white oyster mushroom has very fast-growing mycelium and so is quick to establish. It can be grown outdoors, during summer or winter, with different strains available to suit your growing conditions.

Like all oyster mushrooms, the white oyster belongs to the saprotrophic 'decomposer' class of mushroom (see page 37) and will readily grow on straw, used coffee or hardwood mulch. As a side fruiting mushroom, it is particularly suitable for the straw-bale growing method (see page 92).

It has a subtle umami flavour, and its meaty cap and stem make it an ideal addition to a hearty meal.

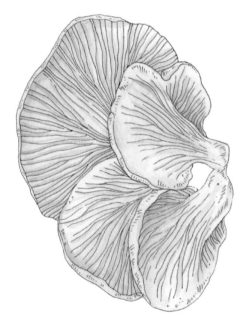

Italian oyster mushrooms

Pleurotus pulmonarius

This delicately gilled mushroom with small, pale caps is part of the oyster mushroom genus that thrives in temperate forests. The Italian oyster mushroom, which is also known as the phoenix mushroom, prefers warm environments and will grow on a variety of hardwoods and some conifers.

It is a great beginner's mushroom for growing: on hardwood logs using the dowel method (see page 86); on straw bales (see page 92); in straw beds (see page 104); and in greenhouses and polytunnels (see page 100). It will fruit through the summer if kept watered and in a shaded area.

Being similar to the grey oyster mushroom, it has a mild and classic mushroom flavour.

King stropharia mushrooms

Stropharia rugosoannulata

These garden giants, also known as wine-cap mushrooms, can grow more than 15–20cm (6–8in) wide. Their deep burgundy caps and pale stems can be found fruiting across Europe and North America throughout autumn. The king stropharia is a ground-dwelling, adaptable mushroom that can be easily grown on beds of leaf litter, straw or mulch (see page 108).

With its firm, pale flesh, this mushroom is especially delicious when cooked and enjoyed on their own.

Turkey tail mushrooms

Trametes versicolor

Turkey tail is a stunning polypore mushroom with multicoloured layers of brown, purple, blue and even green tones, similar to that of the tail on a wild turkey bird. It's a small, stalkless bracket fungus that grows in large clusters on the bark or stumps of hardwood trees across the globe.

Being known for its medicinal benefits, turkey tail has been consumed for its healing properties for thousands of years (see page 184). It should not be confused with the poisonous false turkey tail (*Stereum ostrea*).

Turkey tail can be grown outdoors on almost any type of hardwood, using either the dowel method (see page 86) or by stacking large hardwood discs with layers of sawdust spawn (see page 120). It will need to grow in a weather-protected, shady spot and have regular watering.

We do not recommend eating turkey tail mushrooms as they have a tough, leathery texture, but they can be dried and used in teas (see pages 146 and 150) and tinctures (see page 138).

Wild Growing Mushrooms

Taking yourself out for a mushroom-spotting foray can be wonderful for both your mental and physical health. It's such a good opportunity to open your eyes to the vast variety of fungi growing in natural and built-up spaces in your local area.

Here we share some of the exciting mushrooms you could come across when out walking. While we have listed mostly edible mushrooms, please note many of them have not-so-edible lookalikes. The best introduction to wild mushrooms is a guided walk with an experienced forager. If you aren't completely sure about the type of mushrooms you have found, you should never eat them. No mushroom is worth risking your health for. Always crosscheck all parts of the mushroom, from its cap, stem, spores and underside to its flesh and smell. An experienced guide will detail the similarities between edible and poisonous mushroom, and even the most experienced foragers will have their concerns on occasion. If in doubt, leave it. Happy hunting!

Honey mushrooms

Armillaria mellea

A fascinating mushroom, the honey or honey fungus mushroom is one of a few white-rot fungi that can kill the trees it grows on. You can recognize these fascinating mushrooms by their honey yellow to light brown colouring and the small, shiny, round caps that begin to flatten out as they mature. They are also sticky to the touch. Take particular care not to mistake them for the poisonous funeral bell mushroom (*Galerina marginata*).

As well as growing in large clusters at the base of living, dead or dying trees, honey mushrooms can be found on roots hidden beneath grass, too.

Harvest honey mushrooms when young, and remove the stems. The caps have a good flavour and are great for frying, sautéing and adding to soups.

Jelly ear mushrooms

Auricularia auricula-judae

Also known as wood ear mushrooms, these dark to light brown mushrooms, have a smooth and undulating form and, as their name suggests, can resemble the shape of an ear. When dried, they can also look like a leathery cloth.

Jelly ear mushrooms grow downwards, year-round, on deciduous trees – typically elder (*Sambucus*) – in temperate forests and are most likely to be found after damp and humid spells.

Despite the name of jelly ear, it has a crunchy texture. Its mild flavour is perfect for accompanying stronger flavours: we've even seen it used in homemade Jaffa cakes! Always cook well before eating.

Porcini mushrooms

Boletus edulis

The porcini or penny bun mushroom has a thick, pale stem with a distinctive net patterning and a bulbus cap with a wonderful sheen. The underside is a spore sponge.

Found in the northern hemisphere in broadleaved coniferous and deciduous forests during the autumn, porcini mushrooms grow up from the forest floor near pine and chestnut trees. A popular mushroom, the porcini mushroom is largely foraged as they're difficult to cultivate, due to the nature of their symbiotic relationship with particular trees.

Porcini mushrooms have a deep, woody and earthy flavours that enhance any dish. With a firm texture when cooked, they are particularly beloved by chefs.

Puffball mushrooms

Calvatia spp.

This is one of the first mushrooms to appear towards the end of summer and can be found in deciduous woodlands or on cut grasslands and sports fields. Its distinctive, round, white cap can grow to the size of a football, although it more commonly tops out at the size of a golf ball.

As the puffball begins to mature, its flesh and skin begin to turn an off-brown colour. A mature puffball is quite delicate, with the cap turning papery; when squeezed, the fine spawn dust inside puffs out of the top like a cloud, dispersing in the wind.

Puffball mushrooms are best harvested when young and still white inside and out, with a soft and spongy texture. Avoid any that show signs of yellowing or browning on the outside and inside. Slice the young puffballs, fry and serve on toast with a little seasoning.

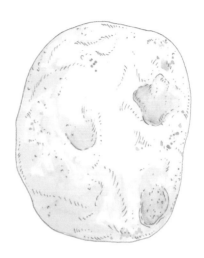

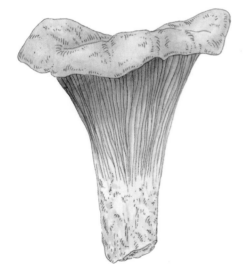

Chanterelle mushrooms

Cantharellus cibarius

The chanterelle has an irregular-shaped cap that turns upwards when mature. With stunning, forked gills that taper down the stem, this classic yellow mushroom is an easy spot. The chanterelle can be found near beech and birch (*Betula*) trees, often growing out of a bed of moss, in woodlands.

Being a mushroom highly prized for its flavour, the chanterelle is very popular – we suggest harvesting only what you need it, and leaving some for the forest and other foragers, too. Its gorgeous, white flesh is a delectable standalone snack or accompaniment to pasta. Do double check if you're harvesting them, that it is not the poisonous false chanterelle.

Dryad's saddle mushrooms

Cerioporus squamosus

A bracket fungus, found on hardwood trees across the world, is also known as pheasant's back because of its unique cap markings. When fully grown, this fungus can reach considerable sizes.

Dryad's saddle is best harvested when young as it can become tough when mature; the stem can be woody so is best thrown away. When young, the succulent white flesh has a slightly sweet aroma that becomes more earthy as it matures. This is a good mushroom to dry and use as a powder (see Mushroom Powder, page 154) or to make stock.

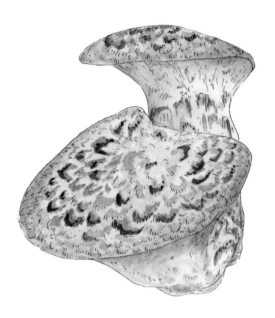

Wood blewit mushrooms

Clitocybe nuda

A distinctive mushroom the wood blewit has a lilac or pink-purple cap, whose tones extend down the stem and on to the gills. As the mushroom matures, the cap flattens out before eventually turning upwards. Unusually, it has quite a sweet odour; some even say it smells like orange juice.

Wood blewit can be found growing in dense woodlands and coniferous forests in Europe and North America, where it is native. It grows off decaying leaf litter from autumn through to winter.

This flavoursome and meaty mushroom is good sautéed in butter or added to an omelette or fried rice.

Mica inkcap mushrooms

Coprinellus micaceus

Characterized by its tawny brown, bell-shaped cap and densely packed gills, the mica inkcap is a saprotrophic mushroom (see Saprotrophs, page 37). Saprotophs thrive on soil and dead or dying wood, though the mica inkcap is very common and not too fussy so is often found growing at the base of trees, as well as in rural areas and towns. It usually grows in dense clusters.

The mica inkcap is closely related to the Shaggy mane mushroom (see page 171), and can be found fruiting in spring, summer and autumn. It will often pop up after a damp spell in mild weather.

This inkcap will rapidly decompose on harvesting, turning black and inky.

Black trumpet mushrooms

Craterellus cornucopioides

The delicate form of these dark grey/black mushrooms, which are also known as horn of plenty mushrooms or black chantarelle mushrooms, can be difficult to spot against the forest floor. They're thin and funnel-shaped, and can have a smooth or wrinkled texture.

Black trumpet mushrooms are found growing across Europe, North America and Asia, among beech, oak and other deciduous trees, throughout the mushroom season until the end of autumn, when the weather begins to cool. They can be easily dried and have a strong flavour, adding a distinctive umami tone to any meal.

King Alfred's cake mushrooms

Daldinia concentrica

It is believed the common name of these mushrooms is derived from the tale of King Alfred the Great, a Saxon king of England, who fled from the Vikings after the Battle of Chippenham. He took refuge in the home of a peasant woman who, unaware of his identity, left him to watch the cakes she was cooking on the fire. Preoccupied with the woes of his kingdom, Alfred accidentally let the cakes burn – they ended up resembling coal pieces rather than freshly baked buns.

An inedible mushroom, also known as coal fungus because of its texture and appearance, it is widely used as a form of tinder for lighting fires. It is dense and dry, and when cut or broken in half, reveals growth rings. If kept dry, King Alfred's cakes can be slow burning and will smoulder for quite a while. They are a slow-growing mushrooms that grow all year-round on dead ash trees or living beech trees.

Birch polypore mushrooms

Fomitopsis betulina

Birch trees are the almost exclusive hosts for this stunning and fairly common bracket fungus, which is a relatively slow-growing mushroom. It can be found growing year-round, and will last well over a year if left undisturbed. When it first appears, birch polypore is often white and stands out against the tree bark, before turning grey/brownish with size and age.

When harvested young and still tender, the mushroom can be sliced and marinated before cooking. It's more often steeped in water to extract its medicinal properties, or dried and turned into powder. Beyond its edible and medicinal properties, the fibrous qualities of birch polypore mushrooms are great for turning into a pulp and making into paper (see page 56).

Hedgehog mushrooms
Hydnum repandum

This mushroom's interesting characteristic is its fine, pale spines that cover the underside of the cap. The top is typically light brown in colour, and tends to be irregular in form.

The hedgehog mushroom is a mycorrhizal fungus (see page 36) found growing near birch, pine or beech trees in coniferous or deciduous woodlands across Europe. As it does not rely on rain, it will fruit once temperatures drop in late summer and can often be found growing in the formation of the classic 'fairy ring'.

This mushroom is best harvested when young, as it can become bitter with age. It's known for its sweet nutty flavour and crunchy texture when cooked. We recommend removing the spines before cooking.

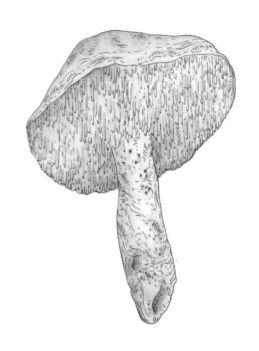

Chaga
Inonotus obliquus

Chaga is a parasitic fungus that infects hardwood trees. Its enzymes decompose the wood and use the nutrients to grow – its sclerotium (a mass of black mycelium) known as the conk, starts to protrude from the tree during later stages of growth.

The tough, slow-growing chaga, which is also known as cinder conk, is most commonly found on birch trees, and thrives in colder climates. The mycelium is dark in colour, mostly black, and resembles charcoal due to high levels of melanin.

Known for its antioxidant, anti-inflammatory and immunity boosting properties. It's best consumed as a tincture (see page 138), which you can create through hot water extraction, alcohol extraction or both. It can also be dried and turned into a powder and incorporated into foods or hot drinks (see pages 136–59).

Slippery Jack mushrooms

Suillus luteus

A member of the bolete family, the slippery Jack is a brown-capped mushroom with a porous underside and pale stem. It's often found growing on the floors of dense pine woodlands or forests. It enjoys a steady temperate climate and will appear in late summer and autumn, while the weather is still mild but damp.

When preparing slippery Jacks, it is highly recommended that you remove the slimy skins before cooking. These mushrooms go well in stews, left whole, peeled and dry sautéed, or simply fried with a little garlic and seasoning. They do not have a particularly strong flavour.

Author's note on safety

When foraging for wild food, you must be able to correctly identify what you are picking, otherwise you should not eat it. Never eat any wild food without multiple sources of positive identification – do not eat any mushrooms just from reading this book. Many edible fungi have lookalikes which may be poisonous. Likewise, not all medicinal products derived from fungi are safe. Please pick responsibly.

Disclaimer

Index and Acknowledgements

Index

Acknowledgements

Mushroom farming wasn't where we imagined ourselves just 5 years ago. As parents to young families, and working in industries that didn't wholly support the change in our personal circumstances, we were constantly on the lookout for an alternative. For something we could still excel in, be proud of, and that ultimately, would work around school runs and summer holidays.

We joke that we gave up our 9–5s to work 24/7 – but mushroom farming has given us a flexible business that is driven by a passion for something we deeply believe in, and we couldn't have done it if it wasn't for some very important people in our lives.

Our journey into mushroom growing has allowed us to meet some incredibly inspirational people who have held our hands, opened doors and led us into spaces we'd never even dreamed of. Here's a special thank you to everyone who's contributed toward this very special book – Arit Anderson, Hélèna Dove, Adam Johnson for his ceramics, Adrian Ogden of Gourmet Mushrooms, Craig from Marvellous Mushrooms, Cultivate London and The Salopian Gardens, photographer Nicky Allen, the team and community from GroCycle, Sarah and Hugh of Applesham farm and Lauren for everything. Not forgetting our friends and family that have willingly been test subjects and sounding boards for our ideas and new projects.

To our dearly missed parents for instilling in us a 'can do – just because we don't know how, won't let that stop us' attitude. To our Dad for imparting to us practical skills and to our Mum, for she never towed the line or followed the crowd. We feel the fear and we do it anyway, which has given us the power to push

ourselves; continuing to continuing to say 'yes' to everything and working out the 'how' later.

To our younger brother, Nigel, for being there at the beginning with his practical support and growing enthusiasm; we descended upon him with our kids and ideas and set up our first grow space in his garage. We're very proud of what he's achieved.

To our families who have supported, pushed and celebrated with us along the way – for their pride, belief and hot dinners.

Lastly, we want to thank each other – as sisters, friends and business partners. As a duo, one of us is always the counter weight for all our seemingly ridiculous and eager ideas, balancing out the other with the practicalities and a spreadsheet or two, while the other is steaming ahead with a passionate enthusiasm, and pie in the sky ideas. But always we're together and there to hold each other's hand when stage fright or imposter syndrome set in.

Life is a learning journey, and I'm so thankful to be on this journey with you.

Here's to finding your thing in your 40s; women empowering women and delving deeper into the mushroom rabbit hole. This book is about sharing all that we have learnt with those who are as excited by the magic of mushrooms as we are.

Lorraine & Jodie.

Quarto

First published in 2024 by Frances Lincoln
an imprint of The Quarto Group.
One Triptych Place, London, SE1 9SH
United Kingdom
T (0)20 7700 6700
www.Quarto.com

ISBN 978-0-7112-8907-9
EBOOK ISBN 978-0-7112-8908-6

10 9 8 7 6 5 4 3 2

Art Director Paileen Currie
Editor Charlotte Frost
Illustrator Katie Putt
Photographer Nicky Allen
Project Editors Anna Watson and Philippa Wilkinson
Publisher Philip Cooper
Senior Commissioning Editor Alice Graham
Senior Designer Renata Latipova
Senior Production Controller Eliza Walsh

Cover image Courtesy of Getty/HQPhotos
p.7, 15 and 16 images coutesy of Caley Brothers.
p.38 Courtesy of Getty/Jakob Valling
p.86 Courtesy of Shutterstock/MN Studio
p.105 Courtesy of Shutterstock/Coulanges
p.124 Courtesy of Getty/ilyasov
p.125–127 Method courtesy of Adrian Ogden of Gourmet
Woodland Mushrooms www.gourmetmushrooms.co.uk

Printed in China

MIX
Paper | Supporting
responsible forestry
FSC® C016973